T0129992

THE CONSCIOUS RELATIONSHIP OF I AND MYSELF

The Game Of Life

G Y A N .

BALBOA.
PRESS

A DIVISION OF HAY HOUSE

Balboa Press books may be ordered through booksellers or by contacting:

Balboa Press
A Division of Hay House
1663 Liberty Drive
Bloomington, IN 47403
www.balboapress.com.au
1 (877) 407-4847

Because of the dynamic nature of the Internet, any web addresses or
links contained in this book may have changed since publication and
may no longer be valid. The views expressed in this work are solely those
of the author and do not necessarily reflect the views of the publisher,
and the publisher hereby disclaims any responsibility for them.

The author of this book does not dispense medical advice or prescribe the use
of any technique as a form of treatment for physical, emotional, or medical
problems without the advice of a physician, either directly or indirectly. The
intent of the author is only to offer information of a general nature to help
you in your quest for emotional and spiritual well-being. In the event you use
any of the information in this book for yourself, which is your constitutional
right, the author and the publisher assume no responsibility for your actions.

Any people depicted in stock imagery provided by Thinkstock are
models, and such images are being used for illustrative purposes only.
Certain stock imagery © Thinkstock.

Print information available on the last page.

ISBN: 978-1-5043-0205-0 (sc)
ISBN: 978-1-5043-0206-7 (e)

Balboa Press rev. date: 04/20/2016

This story is dedicated to all of humanity in the hope that we can all learn, as unique individuals, to work together by doing something for ourselves that is always of benefit to the whole.

PREFACE

Why? I can remember getting into so much trouble as a child, not only at home but also at school for that little one-word question. I knew that there was more to life than I was being shown or was being told which made my question everything, I was often caned at school for asking questions that I now understand my teachers, especially my religious teachers couldn't answer. I was also called stupid and lazy something else I knew wasn't true I had a sharp mind and an excellent memory; although my reading and writing often let me down. It wasn't until the last year of primary school that I was diagnosed with dyslexia but by then I'd had enough of education. The older I got, the more disillusioned I became with life often feeling as if I was from another planet or time period, and so like many disillusioned people I turned to drugs and alcohol; but the answers to life weren't to be found there either.

I also tried travelling, visiting many northern European countries in the hope of finding that part of my life that was missing. Whatever it was that was missing, it seemed to remain just out of reach, and the hole only got bigger until my life felt like I was a hamster on a wheel; running for my life but getting nowhere. In 1988 at the age of twenty-nine I bought a one-way ticket to India in the hope of getting away from my alcohol and drug-fuelled existence. It wasn't as if I was running away from anything; it was more like I was running towards something even though I still had no idea what that was. As soon as I stepped off the plane at Mumbai airport I had the strangest feeling that I had arrived home; I would spend just over six out of the next eight years in India. The question of why still burned brightly and I would spend a lot of my time visiting temples and talking to Brahmin priests asking those same questions that had haunted me for so long of who, what, and why we are here. I also read some English translations of the Vedas and some of the other Indian classics; I found the kind of spiritual connection here in India that I had been searching for that I knew still existed, and although I was for the most part happy there was still a big hole in my life. Then in 1996, I had an experience that made me question my reason for being alive again. Why was I here, what was the meaning of life, and why was mine once again filled with so much sorrow and sadness. I felt that life had given up on me, that it had turned against me once again and had taken away everything of value and was now doing everything that it could to destroy what I had left. The more I questioned what life was, the more I began to wonder what death was and if it could be any worse than the life I was now living. I was so angry at the world that I lived in, religion, society, people in general, in fact almost everything about being alive annoyed me, so I decided just to stop eating and see what would happen.

It wasn't long before I became sick, It started with a fever; probably from not boiling the river water, but I no longer cared if I lived or died. More than a week had passed without me eating any real food, and by now I was finding it hard to keep anything down, even water. At the time, I was staying in Hampi in Karnataka with some friends, but I mentioned nothing to them about how I was feeling or my fever, my travelling companions had decided to head back to Anjuna Beach in Goa, so I decided to pack up and head back with them. It was a gruelling two-day motorbike ride to Goa, and when we arrived, I didn't even have the strength to put my Enfield on its stand and collapsed on the floor of sheer exhaustion. The following morning one of my friends brought me a glass of water, but as soon as the water hit my stomach it came straight back up along with some fluro green slime. My friends realised that something was seriously wrong with me and tried to persuade me to go to the hospital or at least to a doctor, but I refused. Somebody mentioned that Bhan had just arrived in Anjuna beach Goa, Bhan was this seventy-six-year-old Vedic acupuncturist who had helped me before with some health problems, and as he was a good friend I was persuaded to go to his clinic. Upon my arrival, Bhan had a bed ready. Bhan talked with me a little about what was going on with my life; I told that I didn't really want any help I just wanted to lie here and see what would happen.

Bhan said he would honour my request and wouldn't do anything without my approval, although he did persuade me to have acupuncture and drink some herbs to help with the pain that was now ravaging my body.

Within less than six weeks I had gone from a healthy seventy kilos down to around forty-two kilos, I found it hard to stand and even to sit up was starting to become difficult as my body was in so much pain. Bhan told me that my body was starting to shut down, and my liver and kidney function was starting to fail, that my body was starting to eat itself to stay alive. I knew that I was slowly killing myself, but I didn't care; I just lay there waiting for the end.

Then one night in mid-April around Six or seven weeks since I had decided just to give up on life, I had what I believe was a near death experience; it was the light at the end of the tunnel experience. My withered body was lying there in the hammock, and I knew it was no longer me, I was free. I was now everything and nothing at the same time, the closest explanation I can give is that I was pure consciousness. I no longer had a physical body; there was no pain or sorrow anymore, it was as if I was one with everything. I have had out of body experiences before; quite a few in the last two weeks, but this experience was different it was more real than any dream or any waking experience I have ever had or have ever had since. Questions and answers happened simultaneously, time and distance was irrelevant, and the question of why had finally ceased.

I don't know how long the experience lasted; it could have been minutes or hours. Then there was a voice, but no sound or words were spoken, it was more of a sense or understanding, but I knew if I didn't return to my body soon that I would have to remain here, and so I consciously chose to return. I could see my lifeless body there in the hammock on the clinic veranda, and moved over to it and started to merge with it once again. It felt like I was putting on a wetsuit that was two sizes too small, then pop, I was in and at that precise moment the sun rose on the horizon, and I had never felt so alive in all my life.

I felt like a newborn child the whole world was filled with wonder and excitement again; it was as if I was experiencing everything as if for the first time. I have tried on numerous occasions to write about that April night in 1996, but I have never found the words to express where I went and what I experienced other than to say, I went home, and experienced the pure consciousness that I am.

Bhan the old healer who had been taking care of me walked outside a few moments later took one look at me and said, finally samadhi, he told me that I had reached the highest state of consciousness, the state of oneness with the universe. There was so much I wanted to say to him, but the words just wouldn't come out. There was nothing that I could say that could express the understanding of my sense of connection that I was now living, I could still feel the oneness, and finally; I had all my answers and no more questions. I stayed with Bhan for a few more weeks regaining my strength. He gave me special herbs and Vedic potion's along with some 24 karat gold acupuncture needles showing me where to use them and at what time of the day to get the most out of them, I then set out on the next chapter of my life.

During the whole experience, there was this three-word sentence that kept coming into my awareness; those three words were pure, inner, sense. I knew that they had a special meaning to me, after all, I heard them in both my waking and dream states. I would also see them written on walls and signposts in my out of body experiences, and they were communicated to me during my near death experience by the voice with no sound or words. As I had just had a kind of rebirth, I had pure, inner, sense, translated into Sanskrit and decided that Anta Gyan would be my new name believing this to be my new life path; to find a way to work with my pure inner sense.

I decided to leave India and my past behind and move to Australia a country I had wanted to go to since my childhood back in England. Once there I would begin my life again as this new person, Anta Gyan. It was time for the new chapter to begin.

Starting a new life has its challenges especially when some of my choices were based on my past actions. I spent the first seven years reliving my past and ending up in a very similar situation to the one that had made me almost give up on life. I spent far too much time talking about what I was going to do that it used up all my energy, and I started to revert to the angry and bitter person I had left behind. It took me the best part of 16 years to fully understand the experience of that April night in 1996 and to find a way to bring that state of pure inner sense into my daily interactions. I realised that it was my responsibility for the way my life was. My life had come full circle once again, and I didn't like who I had become, memories of Bhan and my time at his clinic started flooding into my waking and dream states again, and the promises I had made to Myself, it was then I realised I was only Anta Gyan in name. I was saying I am Gyan, but I was not being Gyan

It was time to stop talking and start acting. I began offering free Reiki and Tarot readings again and found some work with a voluntary organisation. I remembered the kind of person I wanted to be and simply started acting as if I was that person.

Around 2010 I started to tell my story publicly, firstly at a self-help discussion group I ran out of my flat in Lismore, then I gave some talks at the Byron Sophia, a theosophical study group in Byron Bay. The first talk I gave was on the concept of I and Myself, and it was well received, and I was asked return to give more talks. I was asked by a number of people if I had written a book around my concepts when I said no I was questioned as to why not. In 2012, I moved to Cairns in Far North Queensland and started doing voluntary work at the Cairns Spiritual Centre, using my story, along with Reiki, Pranic healing, Tarot, N.L.P and a few other modalities I had picked up along the way to help people recognise that connection that was always there. I also help facilitate the Mind, Body & Soul group; a Self-help discussion group here in Cairns.

Over the past few years, I have seen firsthand how putting into practice the story of The Conscious Relationship of I And Myself has changed not only my life but the people around me who have taken up the challenge of not just talking about it but actually doing it for themselves. So in 2015 after many years of being asked, when are you going to write a book, I took up that challenge and The Conscious Relationship Of I And Myself came into being.

The Conscious Relationship Of I And Myself is based on the understandings that I brought back with me from my healing crisis; it is my understanding of the oneness of the universe. The conscious relationship is about the individual physical interaction between I this body called Gyan and Myself the complete consciousness of everything as a whole; which includes Gyan. Myself is the best explanation that I can come up with that expresses what that sense of oneness represents to me.

Because where I came from, where I am right now and to where I will return when this body is no more, are all one and the same space; I came from myself, and will return to myself, and I am always in a relationship with myself.

The story in this book will not change your life, and that was never my intention when I wrote it, it is merely my personal perception of life. Who I am now is not the same person that wrote this because everything is constantly changing, and that is why it is written the way it is, just as a story.

I don't believe I am a walk-in, and I am certainly no more special than anybody else, what I know and understand to be true, is true, but only for me. We are each created as a unique individual, and perhaps it's now time for humanity to wake up to that fact and for each of us to take personal responsibility for our own interactions and relationships. The Conscious Relationship Of I And Myself is my story based on my personal experiences and interactions of how that might be possible.

As a story which is an account of imaginary or real people and events told for entertainment, there is no truth in this story only possibilities. The truth or the true secret behind this story you must find for yourselves. The story must be acted out by you in all of your relationships, only then will the secret message from consciousness be understood. Only through the use of knowledge comes understanding.

Knowledge feeds the brain; understanding feeds the whole.

Gyan.

ACKNOWLEDGEMENT

I am truly grateful to every person that I have ever met or will ever meet, without you, I would not be the person I am today.

A special thank you to my mother and father, without your love for each other, I wouldn't be here in the first place.

INTRODUCTION

Modern science proposes that we live in a conscious universe, and everything in the universe is interconnected and interactive.

The Conscious Relationship Of I And Myself is a story told from the viewpoint of Aran a sixteen-year-old who is being interviewed on a radio show about his take on who, what and why we are here.

He gives his personal understanding of what consciousness is and its ability to be the creative force behind everything. He explains why everything is a duality; that duality is the unifying energy that binds everything together and why separation is only an idea, not a reality.

He explains that consciousness as pure energy cannot be created or destroyed, making it eternal, and why this consciousness has created within itself a transient form of energy so as to become more aware of itself and so evolve.

How and why all transient energy is temporary, that the pure energy and the transient energy although never being separate from each other are what we call spiritual and physical respectively. The physical and the spiritual represent the eternal conscious relationship of duality, and each unique physical body is a representation of that whole. That the human body as a unique individual being, has been manifest by consciousness as a scientific experiment so consciousness can understand its duality. Each body has been given the ability to work with the pure energy holistically, using unconditional unity, or the transient energy using the atomistic approach where the parts become more important than the whole causing disunity within the whole; this happens because the body now believes it knows better that pure consciousness what existence should be.

This conscious relationship is between, I, this body as a transient energy and, Myself, as the collective consciousness of all things, and how using this simple concept of I and Myself can restore unity in the individual. Also, as all things are connected, it explains how the individual has the innate power to change the world. There is no other; everything means all things without exception. The Conscious Relationship Of I And Myself is a simple story of how you as a unique individual being by putting into practice some of the ideas expressed in this story may be able to recognise your own connection to the source energy and be the holistic Co-creator you were manifest to be. What if you actually had the power to change the world you lived in and your energy of unconditional unity was all that was needed to restore total harmony within the whole of existence?

You are the most powerful person you will ever meet, by understanding the relationship of I and Myself you can realise you are already everything that you have been searching for, you are the key to your happiness.

It is time for you to be the unique individual being of consciousness that you were manifest to be. Don't wait for some saviour, take personal responsibility for all your interactions because you truly are the One in the All, You are The Conscious Relationship Of I And Myself.

With gratitude and unconditional unity to you all.

Gyan …

ABOUT THE AUTHOR

Born on the 17 Dec 1958 in Brighton England to Cyril and Julie Pownall and named Neil Joseph Pownall.

As Neil, he struggled with school work, at ten years old he was diagnosed with dyslexia and it wasn't until he was 30 that he learned to read and write, and it would be another ten years before he would allow anybody else to read anything that he had written. He played truant for the best part of his secondary education and left school at the earliest opportunity without having taken any formal exams. Neil has worked as a welder fabricator, bar manager, demolition foreman, factory worker and leather worker; he has also had problems with alcohol and drug abuse.

He left England in 1988 with the intention of never returning; In India in 1996 after a life-threatening episode that almost ended his life, Neil changed his name to Gyan, moved to Australia. He has two beautiful daughters Azur and Rhianna from two relationships, and had been married twice.

Since 2006 Gyan has been a citizen of Australia, he has qualifications in Advanced Ericksonian Hypnosis, and Neuro-Linguistic Programming, he also practices Reiki, Pranic Healing and Tarot, along with other modalities he has acquired throughout his travels, he spends three days a week doing voluntary work as a holistic therapist.

Gyan now lives with Rhianna, his 15-year-old daughter in Cairns, Far North Queensland. Having finally understood and put into practice the secret to life that had eluded him for so many years, Gyan has recognised it is of far more benefit to the unique individual to serve the whole than to try and create a reality that only serves the I.

CHAPTER ONE

ARAN STARR

This is my story.

The word story means an account of imaginary or real people, places and events told for entertainment. I am not trying to prove anything to you or change you as that isn't why I'm here, that's your job. It is just a story of how life is from my point of view.

Each one of us is born a unique independent individual, and perhaps it's now time to start acting as such. It's your choice how you experience life; we all have the ability to operate with autonomy, the right or condition of self-governance, and to be responsible for our choices and our capacity to act without conflict for the betterment of humanity regardless of what anybody else is doing. In many belief systems there is the idea we are all born equal; so I would like to start by saying that I don't know more or less than anybody else, I just know different things, and it is in the sharing of our differences that we can learn to recognise our similarities.

Each one of us has our story to tell, and as each one of us has a unique experience or perception of life, then each and every story is valid.

My story is in part about humanity, the fact that we are all one seeing how the word humanity means all humans collectively. We are all created equal, and it is all of humanity that has to evolve together because to think that only some of us are worthy of growing is to work against our true nature of unity. Remember humanity means human beings collectively. There is no truth in the story because it's just words and you all understand that words can and often do mean very different things to different people. The real truth is not just believing the words written here; the real truth comes to you by putting into practice that which has been implied. Only through experience can true understanding be created, only through understanding are we able to glimpse the truth. There is, however, a secret behind this story, but you can only find it for yourselves, It cannot be expressed in words because, if I could tell you, it would no longer be a secret. If you want to find the secret, then all you have to do is put into practice the ideas that are being expressed or implied here.

My story begins with a car crash, and a baby rushed to an incubator after being delivered by caesarean section. The mother had died along with his father in the accident less than an hour before, and there wasn't much hope for the boys survival. The hospital staff were doing everything in their power to give him a fighting chance, and after the baby had stabilised, he was put in an incubator and placed in the intensive care unit. Not longer after the alarms sounded in the I. C. U.; the child had stopped breathing, and his heart had stopped beating. The doctors rushed to his side and tried every technique they could to revive him, after 20 minutes he was pronounced dead. The machines were switched off; the baby washed and carefully wrapped in a soft blanket was taken down to the morgue.

This is the point where I enter into the story; I am now that baby.

The nurse who's name was Sophia Starr then placed the body gently on the table and turned to leave; she stopped just before the door because of something she heard. She quickly turned and looked around the room unable to fully understand what she had just heard and was now seeing.

A wave of both fear and excitement washed over her as she rushed to my side, but once she leaned over I stopped crying and smiled as tears began flowing down her cheeks. She ran over and pressed the panic button and rushed back swooping me up in her arms; I could feel the love pouring out of her as she held me tight against her body. The doctors came rushing in and were amazed at my recovery having thought that I had little to no chance of survival from the moment of birth. After performing all the tests they could think of, I was taken back to the I. C. U. and placed under observation for the next few days.

Within hours the news of the miraculous recovery was abuzz all over the hospital, the newspapers and TV crews were fighting over each other to tell the story, they wrote headlines like "Miracle Baby" and "Baby returns from the other side." Within a week, it had all died down, and they were on to the next big story and mine faded into the past, as do all things. I spent the next two months in the hospital and slowly began to adapt to my new incarnation. Sophia the nurse who had first held me became my primary carer, and our connection grew strong as I knew it would; as it was no coincidence that she was the one that first held me. Having no mother and father or living relatives to look after me, I was put into care as soon as I was well enough to leave the hospital.

Sophia who had held me so lovingly upon my arrival couldn't have children of her own and after talking to her partner Theo they had decided to foster me and before I was six months old was legally placed into their full-time care.

I am what has been called a walk-in. A conscious being that has returned to this plane of existence without the need of being physically born. The soul of the boy had moved on leaving the body as an empty vessel that was still capable of sustaining life as no physical damage had happened to it in the crash. Walk-Ins are happening far more frequently now that ever before in human history, as tremendous changes are being offered to raise the vibration of the Earth to the next level. As walk-Ins, we are here to help humanity with this transition to the next level of consciousness in this never ending experience expressed as life. Being a walk-in, I am here without being conditioned by birth as a physical being; this allows me to inhabit this physical body without the attachment of it being who or what I am. This doesn't mean that I'm a better person than you or more special in any way whatsoever because whatever I can sense, and understand so can you. It is only your attachment to this physical body as yours that is holding you back from sensing the world as I do. Not being conditioned by the birth process allows me a greater awareness of the connection of all things making it easier to understand that where I came from, where I am now and where I am going, are all one and the same space. That everything is from the same source that it is all one and there truly is no other.

Humanity cannot move forward unless we all go together, the very idea that some people are more advanced than others or are more deserving causes most if not all the conflict and suffering on this planet.

I'm getting a little ahead of myself, so I will get back to the story, and we can go into this line of thought later on.

My story is based on the idea of a conscious duality, which to me is the expression of opposites working in harmony forming a consistent and pleasing whole. The word consciousness means, the state of being aware of and responsive to one's surroundings. Implying it is a duality; as there is the part that is aware and the part, it is reactive towards, giving it a dual nature. In this story duality has nothing to do with being separate and everything to do with unity, which means, the state of being united or joined as a whole. The story isn't about one or the other it is about how both these forces form a consistent whole.

I had returned to a physical form to answer the vibrational call for help that had been expressed by humanity, to remind you of something about yourself that you may have forgotten. I also had to learn from an early age that not everyone was ready to hear my story and then one day I had a realisation, my story is just about me as a unique individual body and my relationship and interaction with the whole. I understood how telling this story in the hope of changing others only caused conflict within the whole; which was the opposite reaction to why I started telling the story. So now I tell the story because I am a story teller and what you make of this story is entirely up to you.

I am consciousness, and physical life is the process of consciousness having an experience or relationship of and with itself. Consciousness has created this physical body as a form of a science experiment to understand all the qualities and possibilities within itself, the body being formed from the same source it is experimenting upon always affects the whole with everything that it does. The more physical bodies created within this consciousness, the more individual experiments consciousness, can conduct upon itself simultaneously. Consciousness is the creative source and force of everything without exception, making the physical bodies merely co-creators. The creator and the co-creators cannot and will not ever be separate from each other since there is only one consciousness.

This story is about looking at consciousness and the physical body. How the body co-creates, and why it believes separation to be a reality. How every action I do as a co-creator has an influence upon the whole and the power that is innate within each body to change the world they inhabit.

When I remember my connection to the whole, I am one with all things.

CHAPTER TWO

COMING OF AGE

It was around my 16 birthday that Theo and Sophia organised a bar-b-cue at the house. I enjoyed these events as there was always a healthy mix of people and beliefs at Sophia and Theo's gatherings as their friends came from very diverse backgrounds; they also gave me a platform to express myself and the story I liked to tell. The conversations were always conducted with respect for others beliefs, something that both Sophia and Theo had often expressed to me as a way of communicating without conflict. It wasn't long before a deep conversation about the meaning of life began to develop and once again I was being given a chance to express some of my personal beliefs on this subject. There were a few new faces at the bar-b-cue this time, and I had noticed one such person sat with our group. He didn't say much, but I could tell that he was listening intently to everything that was being said.

I heard Sophia announced that the food was ready, and invited everyone to help themselves to the beautiful spread that was laid out on the tables.

The man who had been sat quietly listening was stood behind me in the line up for food; he introduced himself as Michael Brandon.

He told me that he had a radio show called Unitas, which is Latin for One. He said he would like to interview me for his show being impressed by some of the ideas he had just heard. He gave me his card and said for me to give him a call if I was interested. I told him I would talk to Theo and Sophia and would let him know in the next few days.

Both Theo and Sophia thought it was an excellent opportunity and agreed that I should do the interview. They told me that they had invited him hoping that this would transpire from him listening to one of my conversations, they said that his show was on national radio and had a huge audience and that it was one of the top five rated shows on the airwaves. Sophia told me she thought it was now time for me to reach a wider audience and that this would be an excellent launching platform for my story. Sophia also said how over the past few years she had watched me grow into the story, how both her and Theo had noticed that I wasn't just telling the story anymore, that I was now living it completely. How their friends had seen this also and had begun to make the positive changes within themselves realising just how powerful one person can be to bring about change.

After I had finished my food and helped Sophia clear up the tables, I decided to see if Michael was still here. I found him sat under the big fig tree near the swimming hole at the bottom end of the garden and went and sat on the grass next to him.

He was a middle-aged man and of average build, he had a calm and pleasing manner about him, and I felt very comfortable to be in his presence. We passed a few pleasantries and them I told him that I would be grateful for the opportunity to be interviewed on his show and was looking forward to working with him. He said he would get his office to contact me with all the details in the next few days, and was very much looking forward to the interview also.

We didn't speak much for the next half hour or so we just sat together listening to the sound of the water running over the rocks and the wildlife that was surrounding us. Without speaking, we both stood up at the same time, shook hands and made our way back towards the house and the other guests.

Arrangements were finalised with Michaels office, and the date of the first interview was set. Michael had asked if it would be Ok to interview me at the watering hole on Theo and Sophia's property, I agreed, and the interviews were conducted over a three-day period.

What follows is the transcript of those interviews before being edited and going on air. The first Four interviews we talk about some of the challenges we face, and the last Three we talk about some solutions to overcome these challenges. Please remember, this is a story that needs to be acted out to truly be understood.

Ready For Change

Hello and welcome everyone Michael Brandon here with my special guest today on Unitas, Aran Starr. Some of you may know or have heard of Aran as the miracle baby from the news headlines of some sixteen years ago, when after being pronounced dead suddenly came back to life some thirty minutes later at St Joseph's hospital. Aran was later adopted by Sophia and Theo Starr; Sophia was the nurse who had first held him on the day of his miraculous recovery and had named him Aran, which means bringer of light. Sophia recently told me she called him Aran because of his beautiful smile, the first connection she remembers about him and how that smile had lit up her life.

I was invited to a bar-b-cue a few weeks ago by Aran's mother where I overheard a conversation Aran was having with a group of people, and I was fascinated by some of the wisdom that this young man was able to express.

Over the next few weeks here on Unitas we will be enquiring into the meaning of life from Aran's perspective and his personal understanding of who, what, and why we are here.

Welcome, Aran, and thank you for being my guest here today on Unitas.

Aran… Thank you, Michael, it's a pleasure to be here.

Michael… We have only had a few conversations over the past few weeks, but I would have to say that listening to you speak, especially for someone so young, you seem to have a very clear understanding of life and your place in it.

You talk of a world without conflict, a world that is based on unconditional unity and how individually we each have the innate power within us to achieve this goal. You call yourself a storyteller and that you are here to tell your unique story of what it means to be you in your world, so I would like to start by asking, what is your story about and why do you feel the need to tell it?

Aran … The meaning of the word story is an account of imaginary or real people and events told for entertainment. My story is no different, it may or may not be true, but hopefully it will be entertaining. It is my understanding that each person on this earth has been manifest to have a unique experience as a co-creator, and it is about time that we all learned to honour that reason for being here. It is a story of unconditional unity and an elegant way of expressing that unity so the individual can live a life without conflict. My story is no more or less important than any other story, and I am not trying to convince anybody that it is true. There is some truth in it, but to find that truth the story must be acted out, not just talked about. If each person were to act this way with unconditional unity towards everything in their uniquely perceived world, I believe something wonderful can and will happen.

It is up to each person to take up the challenge; it is your choice, and it always has been, nobody can force you to act this way you must decide for yourselves.

Michael … Are you saying that there are some hidden meaning's in this story, and if so what is the message?

Aran … The story is filled with clues, but it is only by putting those clues into practice that the hidden meaning comes into being. If you were to put into practice the ideas and concepts of this story for yourself, you might very well come to your own unique understanding of how to be and how to act holistically towards all life. It is a story of how I as an individual have the possibility to change the world that I inhabit and by doing so how I can change the whole of creation.

My story is basically about the duality of consciousness expressed as the relationship between I and myself. I have come to understand that consciousness is both one thing and everything at the same time, the infinite and the finite, the eternal and the transient. Most of all that consciousness is dual in nature. Duality is the expression of opposites working in harmony creating a pleasing and consistent whole. It is a story about this and that, not, this or that.

Only as human beings do we perceive the world as separate from ourselves and this story offers a way to end this idea of separation, which after all is all that separation is, an idea. It is my personal understand of why consciousness, through the use of its duality, has created this relationship that I have called the game of life, a game that is played between this dual nature of consciousness and that duality is expressed as I and Myself, the finite and the infinite as a complete whole.

Stories have always played an important role in the shaping of humanity; they help us to use our imagination and to think outside the box, to see the world from a different point of view. If this story helps just one person to look and think about the world you live in from a different perspective, then it will have been worth telling. As I have already mentioned this story may or may not be true, but perhaps if you imagined what it would be like if it were true, then something wonderful might happen. Imagination being one of the greatest gifts we possess; it is also the gift that we misuse the most. The reason I say this is because imagination is a mental exercise, it is all happening in the head, and unless what we know is put to use, it is nothing more than a senseless exercise.

Michael ... Can you please explain what you mean by a senseless exercise?

Aran ... When we are only thinking about something, we can and often do dismiss our other senses, and this is what I am implying by being senseless.

Michael ... So your interpretation of senseless is when we don't use all our senses together to make decisions.

Aran ... Yes, that is correct. We imagine a world based on separation and, for the most part, live our lives as if that idea were true, even though modern science has shown us the everything in the universe is interconnected and interactive.

We have become senseless in our thoughts and deeds because only thinking about something doesn't use all of our senses.

For the most part, people live their lives in their heads accepting the stories that have been told to be true without even checking them out for themselves.

Knowledge it would seem in this day and age is king, but this king rules without understanding. In my story knowledge isn't the same as understanding. Knowledge is just the accumulation of information; a library has a vast amount of knowledge contained within it, but, the library isn't going to change anything unless a person puts that information into practice.

Only through putting into practice the knowledge being expressing here will you find the real meaning behind this story.

The earth is at a junction and its time to turn to the right way, the way that benefits everyone and everything as a whole. We have all the knowledge needed to fix every challenge that humanity and the environment are facing both individually and collectively. It is only through our lack of acting holistically, this senseless act, that change is being stifled. To build anything new it first has to have a solid foundation and that foundation starts with You. We each have the innate ability to change the world. You as a unique individual are the most powerful person you will ever meet on this planet because you can change the world. It is a story of a silent and peaceful revolution and the possibility of ending all the conflict not just in your world but all the worlds. I am not here to tell you what to do or how to be; this is just my story of what it means to be me in my world. What anybody else does with their life is entirely up to them.

All that I ask is that if you hear something in this story that might work for you in your own game of life, then give it a try, what do you have to lose.

Michael … I like the idea of a silent and peaceful revolution, is this what you are attempting to teach with your story?

Aran … The silent revolution only happens when I stop talking about what I know needs or has to happen and physically start doing it for myself. It is the same for you; the silent revolution begins when you stop telling others what to do and start doing what you know needs to be done. Just like the library, I can give you some information as to what it means to be me in my world; as I am doing now, but as I mentioned already; only through action comes understanding. So in a sense, each person has to teach themselves, because I am just the storyteller.

Michael … Having heard some of your story Aran, I believe that if more people perceived the world the way you do and acted accordingly things could be much different.

Aran … Each person on this planet perceives the world they live in from a unique individual perspective, I call this, The many worlds theory. So please don't follow me because you will not be living the unique life you were created to have.

My story is just about what it means to be me in my world, a world where everything is interconnected and interactive and how I have managed to recognize that connectedness of all things without exception. I don't believe I'm capable of teaching you to perceive my world, but I know you are capable of teaching yourselves to perceive the connectedness in your own world.

Like I just said I am not trying to convince anybody that you should follow my example, because, if you follow me or try to live in my world you are no longer living your life as the unique individual being you were manifest to be.

Every one of us has a unique story to tell about what it means to be them in the world they inhabit, and I believe that every story is, therefore, worth telling.

We are all storytellers, and every story has some importance in it, especially when it is about your own personal experience of life and how it has made you feel interconnected and whole.

It is by sharing our differences we are able to sense our similarities and rejoin humanity instead of trying to separate it.

Michael ... When you say it is through the sharing of our differences that we are able to see the similarities, could you please give me an example?

Aran ... Theo and Sophia, like to travel, and I have been taken to many different countries over the past sixteen years. Many of these countries have very different beliefs and religions, different food and languages, skin colour and clothing, the more we traveled, the more I began to realise just how similar we all are. Regardless of all these differences, we are all conceived and born the same way, have the same internal organs and body structure; we need food, water, fresh air, companionship and somewhere safe to rest and sleep for our ongoing survival. We all rely on nature and this planet our garden home for all our needs.

The truth is there are far more similarities between us than there are differences, even the fact that we all have our differences makes us similar.

Michael ... How does this all fit into the idea of the many worlds theory?

Aran ... The many worlds theory is based on the idea that each person is born to have a unique experience of life, we all perceive the world differently.

All these worlds are interconnected because they are all manifest from the same source, that source being consciousness.

What happens in one world affects all the others because of this interconnectedness. My story is based upon the responsibility that I as an individual body, called Aran, have towards not only the world I inhabit but also the realisation that what I do as the co-creator of my world really does affect the whole. The more similarities I sense between all these worlds, the less conflict and more cooperation I am likely to have. Similarity is the glue that binds all the worlds together into a unified whole; similarity is still a form of difference. Think of a forest of fir trees where they all look similar but are in fact uniquely individual trees, no two trees are the same, and no two worlds are the same, only similar. This is why it is just about me in my world and how I can learn to have an unconditional relationship with all the other worlds. Difference causes separation, whereas similarity causes a connection.

When I am able to end the conflict in my own world by recognising our similarities and the interconnectedness of everything, it is not just me that benefits but the whole. This foundation for change starts with you the unique individual. What if you are the final world that brings stability to the whole, don't you owe it to yourself and everybody else to at least try, don't just talk about how you are going to change, do it. Join me in the silent revolution.

The many worlds theory means we are all here for a uniquely individual experience, and I recognise that the next step in evolution is a revolution, as in, a dramatic and wide-reaching change in conditions, attitudes, or operation within each of these unique worlds. It is time for the individual to wake up and stop blaming this perceived other for the challenges they recognise in their own world, to take personal responsibility for the world that they inhabit and do what is best for the whole.

Michael … I can accept most of what you have said so far, my next question is, what can I do about these things that I perceive that have nothing to do with me?

Aran … Although you live in your own unique individual world, all the worlds are interconnected and overlap so if you perceive it, it is part of your world. When you deny its a part of your world, you are trying to separate your world and reality from everything else. Separation has been the mentality of the majority for millennia, blaming this perceived other for the challenges that they recognise in their world. You are now the one that is in a conflicting relationship, whether you realise it or not. This form of relating never feels good only because you are trying to do the impossible. You are trying to separate duality.

Michael … I understand that you are just answering my questions, but you also seem to be pointing fingers; isn't what you are saying just your perception.

Aran … Of course, it is. I am not trying to change you or teach you anything; we are just having a conversation here about what may or may not be possible in the world in which we live. It is time though to stop giving away your power by blaming others for your own perceived challenges and once again honour and respect the unique individual you were manifest to be and your unique relationship with the world you inhabit. As a co-creator, you are the cause and the effect of your perceptions, and you cannot perceive something unless it is already a part of you, because everything is interconnected and interactive.

We truly are all one, and it is time to stop thinking in terms of separation, this senseless act of trying to divide consciousness. Consciousness is the source of all things; it is time to remember we are all part of this consciousness and learn to act as such and once again co-create heaven on earth.

Humanity has sent out a message asking for help with these conscious changes that are now being felt in each of your own worlds, many people are waking up to this conscious revolution, and I am simply here to share my story about how I was able to bring about this conscious shift in my world.

Remember; knowing isn't the same as understanding.

There isn't any truth in there words there are only possibilities, So if you hear or read something in my story that you think might work in your world, experiment with it, try it out, what do you have to lose. Remember, although this might sound like science fiction to some of you, science fiction often ends up as science fact once the ideas are put into practice.

Michael … It's true that many people seem to be waking up to the fact that the old ways are no longer serving us as a whole, and a new system is needed.

If I understand you correctly, you're implying this new system is based upon individual action. That it is the individual that holds the key to a more harmonious relationship between all these worlds.

Aran ... Yes, this is a more solid foundation for change. Only when each individual wakes up and takes personal responsibility for the pain and conflict perceived in their own unique world will the revolution be achieved without any contradiction being present. It is time to stop fighting and return to the interconnectedness of all things as an entirely unified whole.

The time of the conscious revolution is at hand, a time where you can stop living in the illusion of separation created by false prophets and return to the reality where all your basic needs are always met, where there is enough of everything for everyone.

Michael ... You just mentioned false prophets, can you explain what or who these false prophets are.

Aran ... There is no denying that we are living in a time of misinformation and deception by those in authority that is leading to further segregation and conflict within the whole of humankind. So in my story, false prophets are anybody or any organisation that is still teaching from a separatist point of view.

I am not blaming these organisations or individuals, after all, we are the ones who believe them without checking out what they say to be factually accurate in the first place. We are also the ones who gave them our authority in the first place to act on our behalf. So any teaching that is exclusive and creates any form of conflict between one side and another is a false prophet.

We are all one, there is no other, everything is interconnected and interactive, we are part of the nature of this planet and cannot survive without its cooperation. Whatever we do, individually or collectively, effect's the whole whether we are aware of this fact or not. Everything is interactive and interconnected your personal vibration makes you a co-creator, when you are happy the whole of creation benefits, when you are sad the whole of creation suffers; this is your innate ability to co-create change. It is the same with any vibration that you emit as a physical body.

The more you try to live in somebody else's reality the more out of balance you become and when you are out of balance all of creation suffers.

Michael … Hold on a minute, are you saying that I have to take personal responsibility for the conflict that I feel in the world.

Aran … If you feel it, then it is part of your world, and, therefore, your responsibility. You read the news on your radio show simply because its part of your job description don't you Michael?

Michael … Yes, that true.

Aran ... You don't know whether that story is real or not because you were not present at the so called incident. Very few of these so called news stories have a positive message in them, in fact, most news coverage is often of a negative nature and is sensationalised in the hope of taking the listener out of their comfort zone and leading them into the fantasy world of imagination.

Most news stories that are told are no longer happening; the stories are about a past event, and it's very challenging to live in the present when you are thinking of the past. So whenever you watch, read or listen to these stories and believe them to be real. You may then talk about them as if they are actually happening right now when in fact they are not. I wonder if you realise you are emitting the vibration that keeps that experience active just by talking about them as if they were real.

When I look at the so-called news on the Tv or the internet and the weekly trash magazines, the headlines are often sensationalised in the hope of luring you out of your world and into their world of fantasy and make-believe.

As an example read these three headlines,

Man gets drunk again and then beats his wife and children.

Woman spends all her money on gambling and children go hungry.

Old woman gets pushed down stairs breaking her arm.

Because these kinds of headlines are expressed as news we are more likely to believe in them, after all, why would the news people lie to us.

We may then, without actually reading the whole story gossip about these people and the headlines by only living in our imagination.

When you are talking about a man who beats his wife and children and whether this story is real or imagined you are emitting a vibration of conflict and violence. An unhealthy misuse of the gift of imagination.

Now read what the story is about beyond the sensationalised headlines.

Man gets drunk again and then beats his wife children at monopoly winning first prize.

Woman spends all her money on gambling and children go hungry until husband comes home with shopping.

Old woman gets pushed down stairs breaking her arm; the youths were praised for saving her life in the horrific house fire.

When I allow myself to be dragged into the illusion of somebody else's world, I am out of time, out of harmony and out of balance with the only world where I actually exist, mine. So to answer your question, words are the biggest of the false prophets simply because we believe in the power of words often without ever checking out for ourselves whether the stories are true. Stories are no longer just told for entertainment, stories especially those that cause a sense of conflict have become the greatest of the false prophets.

Michael … I understand what you're saying about reading the news and how I believe in these stories without me having any physical proof. How the use of gossip is senseless based on what you said earlier about all the senses not being utilised, how gossip is what I imagined happened, but, I am telling the story as if it's a fact. I can also see just how much of life is based on gossip, whether it is a so-called terrorist attack, or merely talking about something we overheard about what happening in somebody else's world that may or may not be true, how this always leads me away from my own world. I think I also understand what you mean by the silent revolution, To be present in this actual moment has little to do with words and everything to do with feelings and sensations.

Aran … We are convinced from a very early age to believe in things that aren't and never have been real, examples of this are; the Easter Bunny, Father Christmas, the tooth fairy, the boogie man, etc. We are conditioned to believe in many things that are not and never have been real.

This kind of story without proof that our guardians, our parents and so called teachers force upon us as being real has led many to such ridicules beliefs that all Muslims are terrorists, blacks are inferior to whites and separation is more important than unity. For the most part, humanity has given away its power to some form of authority, real or imagined, blindly following in the footsteps of those that have gone before. We have for the most part lost sight of our own unique life path, simply because, we are trying to live in the illusion of somebody else's world. Governments, education, and consumerism, are all in need of fundamental changes. The challenge is to create a new system that is based on unity, respect, and harmony for all of humanity, not just the chosen few. The amount of misinformation that is being expressed on a daily basis in the hope of shoring up the old crumbling system is phenomenal.

It is no longer the minority that seeks change, but as a whole, we need to be mindful of how that change is implemented.

Michael … I recognise for myself who these false prophets are, but, I am also beginning to understand how it's not so much their fault for telling the stories as it is mine for being senseless as you just called it and believing in them in the first place without any form of proof. Also that a lot of the so-called news is about past events.

My next question is what are some of the foundations of change you see on the building of these new systems for all societies to unify.

Aran … They are not much different from the ones fundamental to the societies you live in today. Unity, respect, equality, freedom, harmony and community.

Michael … Don't we have these already, how does that make a new system?

Aran … Do you believe that you have these qualities?

Look at this earth that we all live on, do you really see respect, equality and freedom for all, in all walks of life. Do you see people working in harmony with each other and the very nature they are manifest from? The people that create and enforce the laws of the land act in many cases as though they are exempt from those laws. It's not hard to find bankers, politicians, police and religious leaders who are corrupt and if you see your leaders as corrupt is it any wonder that you then learn to become corrupt yourselves.

Michael … So you are saying that everyone is corrupt to some extent?

Aran … One of the dictionary definitions the word corrupt is; having or showing a willingness to act dishonestly in return for money or personal gain. People in this day and age will do almost anything for money just because they are convinced that you cannot live without money. We believe this story that money is everything and allow it to control us, even though money doesn't and never has made the world go round. Money is quite a recent manifestation, it has little to do with the greater good and much to do with self-gain, so yes, we all use some form of corruption every now and again.

Michael … OK, I would have to agree with you on that point.

Aran … Money is in a sense another false prophet isn't it, It is an illusion. We are told we cannot live without it, and so it is used as a tool of control.

Anybody that uses power and force to control an others autonomy is misusing the power that they have been given. This struggle for power whether you feel it as being taken from you or as trying to have it over another is again an action that keeps the individual out of balance. When you act using power and control over another these so-called fundamental foundations of Unity, respect, equality, freedom, harmony and community are not present.

There is nothing wrong with governments, banks, police or religious organisations when they truly work for the people, so it's not about getting rid of anything, it's more about finding a better use of these resources to benefit the whole, not just a few. Everybody that is born on this earth regardless of race, creed, colour, social or political background is a child of this earth, and all deserve an equal share of its bounty. Then and only then will Unity, respect, equality, freedom, harmony and community truly be present in all worlds and we can all return to the garden of Eden.

Michael … How and where do you see these changes beginning?

Aran … It is a grass root revolution because it will have to start with each unique individual taking personal responsibility for their own actions first.

It is about taking back the innate power we have each been given to be a co-creator and to live sustainably on this garden planet that we have been given, where all our basic needs are supplied.

There is enough food produced to feed everyone on the planet yet hundreds of thousands of people go hungry every day.

It is estimated that about one-third of all food production worldwide approximately 1 billion tonnes is lost or wasted every year.

First world consumer rich countries waste almost as much food as the total production of sub-Saharan Africa each year. You are still being told by those in authority that you need to increase food production if you are going to feed the people of the planet. In the country that I live in, which only has population of less than twenty-four million, an estimated five — six billion dollars of food a year, that's around 450,000 garbage trucks of edible food goes to landfill. Twenty - forty percent of all produce is rejected even before it reaches the shop. Worldwide we also feed and then slaughter millions of animals that never make it to the shops let alone the dinner table. All this is happening because of greed and corruption, where numbers on a piece of paper or ones and zeros on a computer have become more important than life itself.

School education teaches for the most part from a reductionist and atomistic point of view where the parts are more important than the whole, and there isn't one single lesson as far as I can see that is based on love and unity. Even religious education only really compares every other religious practice to the one that is prominent in that particular country, whereas the origin of the word religion is to bond or bring together.

The politician's of the world spend most of the time arguing their differences and blaming the other parties for the problems caused, even though they are all involved in one form or another in those same problems. Governments lock people up for fraud and theft, violence and murder, then invade other countries and perpetrate these same atrocities in your name.

I could go on and on about the imbalance in humanity, but that isn't going to help anybody. It is time to wake up and stop this blame game, to stop fighting and take back your authority and act holistically.

By realising you are a co-creator and learning to take responsibility for your world and your world alone you will have taken the first step towards reclaiming your power, the revolution starts with you.

Michael … It's about a new way of doing and being then that benefits the whole and if I'm not mistaken it starts with each individual being. We each have the power to change our own world or, at least, our perception of the world we live in and even as an individual it is about doing what best for the whole.

Aran … Think big, Start small, Learn to work with nature not against it.

Like it or not we are all in this together and remember there is no us and them in humanity.

Unless all humanity can work together with respect, harmony, equality and freedom for all life, it is doomed. Forget about saving the polar bears, or the whales when over fifty-six billion farm animals are killed each year; that doesn't include seafood which is counted in tonnes, around one-hundred-million tonnes a year. It is estimated two-trillion marine animals are fished from the sea alone, and over thirty percent of all these animals and fish are killed needlessly never making it to the dinner table.

Saving humanity from its own self-destruction is the most efficient way to restore balance to our garden home.

Michael … I'm a meat eater Aran, I need meat, I've always eaten meat. I recognise that we kill far more animals than we actually eat and there is a lot of waste, so I hear what you are saying, but, I am just one man what can I do that will make a difference to all this.

Aran … You are not born a meat eater and very few children on this planet actually eat meat in the first two years of your life, in fact, we all start out life in a way as vegetarians. Those first two years signify some of your most significant growth and development of the human body.

We are born natural vegetarians and are then convinced in the belief that you cannot live without meat. Even though those first two crucial years are physical proof that you have and can live without it. Many children that are now being born today are choosing to be vegetarians simply because they don't want to needlessly hurt animals. Their now meat eating parents persuade them they can't do without meat that they need meat to survive, this again has little to do with respect for others belief systems and more to do with controlling them.

I have travelled all over India, and it is estimated that there are over three-hundred-million vegetarians in that country, and statistically they are healthier and live on average for five years longer than their meat-eating counterparts. Don't just believe stories, check them out for yourselves. Ignorance isn't and never has been a reasonable excuse to build a belief upon. It is time for this senseless form of conditioning to stop.

Michael … I never thought of it like that before and your right, my children didn't eat meat for well over two years and in that time they were never sick, we then persuaded them to eat meat simply because we did.

That's really got me thinking now.

Aran … I am not trying to persuade you to become a vegetarian; that has to be a personal choice. The fact is I am not against meat eating, I am only against the needless slaughter of life in any form simply for greed.

I don't want to get into a food debate with you, just point out some fundamental facts, one of those being, if we were only to take what is actually needed for our daily survival we could quickly return our home to a sustainable garden.

Each human physical body is conceived as a successful and integrated part of the whole, and the first nine months of life are a testament to that. In those first few months, you do not ask or want for anything, yet everything is provided at the instant it is required without question.

Even in the first moments after your birth, there is no denying that almost every child is showered with love, affection and gifts, once again a testament to your abundance. You are then taught to let go of your birthright, your sovereignty and abundance and your connection to the whole. You are then conditioned to live in somebody else's reality.

Now you are no longer a success; you have to work at becoming a success. You then spend most of your life out of balance with the very nature that once provided for your every need. Your individuality and your uniqueness, your abundance and connections that you are conceived with now become things you need to work at and find.

Looking for something you already have means that even if you find it, it's hard to recognise it when you come across it. Take abundance for example; how many people have more food in their fridge and cupboards than they can eat today. Also, at the end of the day still have money in their pockets or bank accounts than they needed to spend that day, yet they do not recognise this abundance and keep searching for something they want that they already have.

Michael … It all sounds so simple when you put it like that Aran, and you are right when you say that if we were only to take what was needed for our daily needs, there would be more to go around.

Aran … From my perspective Michael, there is a huge difference between want and need; a need is something that is essential. As a physical being your essential needs are food, water, air, shelter and companionship, and as long as these needs are supplied you could survive almost anywhere on this planet, do you agree?

Michael … Yes, I would have to agree with that statement.

Aran … So anybody listening or reading to this regardless of age is only able to do so because all your essential needs have been met from the moment of conception to this very moment in time. They have been supplied with enough food, water, air, shelter and companionship do you agree?

Michael … Well, If I think about it; then the answer has to be yes.

Aran … This fact of life that regardless of race, creed, social or political background if you are alive right now then all your essential needs have been met. These essential needs that have always been fulfilled are again proof of your success as a living being, yet many people again do not realise this success instead believing success has more to do with the trinkets and the non-essentials of life, ignoring the gifts they have been given by life itself. Wants only come into play when you forget this basic fact of life that what is needed is always supplied.

Want is a desire to possess or wish for something. Do you recognise that if you wish or want, you are expressing the idea that you don't have it?

Learning to be grateful for what you have been given, and the realisation that as long as your daily needs have been supplied you are a success.

You have been given the chance to live another day and to be the person you were manifest to be.

Michael … Listening to you talk and your ideas it would seem to me, at least, that most of my personal challenges could be fixed by literally thinking the opposite to the way I normally think.

Aran... Changing the way you think is a good start. You exist because of duality where both opposing forces are working in harmony to achieve and maintain a pleasing and consistent whole. You have been given what some call free will the innate ability to work with the whole or against it. You have tried working against it and look where that has got you so far, so why not try working with it, what do you have to lose.

Heaven and Hell exist right here on this plane of existence; they are the extreme frequencies of consciousness expressed as the coming together and the moving apart, the expansion and contraction, the vibration of energy as a unified whole.

As members of this garden you too are capable of these extremes of frequency, expressing either unity and love towards, or, separation and fear against this your earth garden home. The garden that humanity was given in which it could take shelter and feed and evolve as a whole or destroy until it is nothing more than a burning planet.

You always have a choice, which kind of world do you want to live in and leave for your children?

Most indigenous tribes believe that they are part of the earth and understand that it is a living being, that you are all deeply connected to it whether you are aware of this fact or not. They also believe they are only the custodians of the land and are here to care for it, to keep it as it was given to them to pass on to their children. To take only what is needed living in harmony with the earth garden which provides for all of their needs. There is no other, humanity and the Earth are one, everything that you do is within the living cell that is your garden home, every action of every individual is part of the co-creation within this living cell, and your basic energies of co-creation are expressed as love and fear.

When you blame others for the disease and unrest that you sense within this living cell of your garden home, it is you that is acting like cancer. This fighting amongst yourselves with these perceived enemies that are not, or so you believe, actually from your garden and must be eradicated at all cost makes you the instigator of conflict. Unable to recognise that this is simply internal conflict between aspects of the garden, humanity fights itself, and it is the garden that suffers.

Michael … If I understand you correctly, you are implying that the human body and the Earth are very similar. That the human body being a community of cells that must all work together holistically to maintain a healthy environment, only becomes diseased, when certain groups of cells believe that their life is more important than the whole as a group. Then looking at the earth as a living cell, it is also only when certain groups think their life is more important than the whole that the earth becomes diseased.

Aran ... Yes, when the internal parts go to war with each other, it is always the whole that suffers. When you blame others for the suffering; you are as much at fault, you become like cancer cells fighting amongst yourselves, and it is the earth and everything within it that suffers. You have for the most part forgotten that you are the caretakers.

The overall belief system that fuels your direction I will call a capitalist system upbringing, which now involves almost the entire population of this earth in some form of monetary exchange for services rendered and corruption is the fuel of this system. This form of corruption perpetrated by the false prophets that life and existence are based on pieces of paper and one's and zero's is the cause of a kind of cancer that is sweeping over our garden home, and we are all suffering the consequences of shoring up a system that is no longer sustainable. Instead of living in harmony with our garden home it is dug up to sell for paper to buy food and shelter with that was once provided freely by your garden home. No longer walking in the garden to forage for your food you have let go of these memories of abundance when all your needs were met by your garden home, you have replaced them with memories of who has what you want and what they want for it, so the concept of lack has come into play. Your true sense of belonging to your garden home and all it contains is no longer part of the collective consciousness of the planet.

Michael ... Do you actually believe we can return to this garden of Eden?

Aran ... We never left, we are in the garden right now. The challenge we face is to learn how to work with the garden again and stop working against it.

Michael ... What do you mean by working with the garden and not against it?

Aran ... Almost every house has a garden, but most of these gardens are devoid of any edible foods, their owners may spend hundreds if not thousands of dollars on maintaining them each year to keep them looking nice. With the same amount of time, effort, and resources some but not all these houses could grow their own vegetables and become self-sustainable; this is not only good for the house owner but the environment.

Michael ... That's a good point, but not everyone has the time or the physical capacity to work in their own garden.

Aran ... This is where the community comes into play; many people like to garden and cultivate food, but can't find work, perhaps you could find someone to maintain you food garden in exchange for a share of the crops.

These are just ideas remember; I am not saying you have to do this.

Michael … It is a very good Idea though Aran, I spend three-hundred dollars a month on my garden and get nothing to eat out of it.

Aran … We were talking about how both possibilities are always present in any situation, and as we have just talked about the garden of Eden lets have a look at heaven and hell. Few people could deny that they have experienced what might be termed heavenly and hellish moments. If you have ever felt like dying through physical or emotional pain you thought would last forever then you know what I mean by a hellish moment.

Heavenly would be something like when you see something born or the moment that you fall in Love, that feeling of being alive that you want to last forever, these are the total extremes of unity and separation.

I wonder how many are aware that this is the biggest lesson that you face as humanity, to manifest heaven or hell here on earth, especially in your own world.

You have for the most part forgotten you are all one integrated whole, you now blame the governments and politicians of the world, these same leaders that you have given your responsibility of care to every election are the ones that allow this destruction to take place in your name. But because you relinquished your responsibility to them, it is no longer your fault, and you are unable to see you are protesting against yourselves. You blame big industry for the pollution, forgetting that without you buying the products they manufacture none of this would be happening. You stopped asking where and how they had acquired what you wanted, just how much they wanted for it. Many have come to fear the very planet that they are a part of to the point that now, for the most part, modern man lives in sterile environments blocking out as much of the outside world as possible.

You fear the germs and bacteria that are already a part of you to the point you now go to war on the garden of our own body. By using chemicals to shave or wax, shampoo and condition, hair straightener and gel, soap and body wash, moisturiser and skin creams, deodorant and perfume, aftershave, makeup, toothpaste, mouthwash. Then there are the bathroom cleaning products most if not all these products now come to you in plastic containers.

Think of the amount of energy and destruction that has been used to generate all this stuff from the garden that isn't essential or necessary for your existence; this is just in the bathroom. Your world is now filled with things inside and outside your homes that have all been made from the garden; some took the garden thousands of years to grow and have been ripped out with such force that they may never grow again. You destroy any part of the garden that can be exploited to produce thousands of objects that are of little to no use for your survival or your basic needs of food, water, fresh air, somewhere safe to sleep and companionship.

You are at war with your very own nature, because, useless items are now of more important that your basic needs.

Man will forever be at war until the lesson of taking personal responsibility and your connection to this garden Earth is restored.

You consciously or unconsciously gave permission for others to act in your best interests and your ability to forgive not only these perceived others for what they have done but also yourself for consciously or unconsciously allowing them to do so in your name is the first step back into the garden.

You are all responsible together, all the collective thoughts since the beginning of mankind's creation within the garden is the thought field manifest, what you all as an individual collective believe it to be.

Imagine ten-thousand people go to watch a game of football; each person has their own unique experience, good, bad or indifferent, together all these emotions create the overall atmosphere. When you blame others for the atmosphere, do you not recognise the part you are playing as a co-creator, this fighting amongst yourselves will only stop when each person takes responsibility for their own personal actions.

It is time to stop blaming others and ourselves for the past mistakes and to realise humanity is out of balance; this is expressed as the chaos in the world at this present time. You want the pollution to stop but still fill your bathrooms and homes with some of the symptoms of the pollution you perceive; you want war to stop by using war and angry protest against your own humanity. You want to feel more connected but are frightened by your fundamental connection to nature;

you want somebody else to be responsible for fixing the challenges that you all face, after all, you didn't cause the damage just purchased the end product. You are unable to see the connection of all things as a whole, and you are indeed heading for a life of Hell on earth for all humanity.

For any garden to flourish a healthy balance ecosystem must be maintained between all the elements of the earth. Humanity is an integrated part of that ecosystem, you never were, have been or ever will be separate from it. You as consciousness chose to incarnate, to become living members of the earth. Through the use of these bodies created of the earth, taking back this responsibility for the life of which you are now conscious and only taking what it necessary for your personal existence, becoming more mindful of your own personal impact on your environment and seeking more sustainable ways to exist.

The garden of Eden is a state of mind; it can be Heavenly or Hellish, you individually choose based on your own perception and belief which of these states to express.

Michael … I hear what you are saying, but we can't go backwards to being hunter-gatherers. I agree that we do produce an enormous amount of things that are of little use that inevitably end up as landfill, often within days of them being purchased, so are you saying the sustainability has to start with the individual.

Aran … In my story yes it does. Earlier on you mentioned that perhaps your personal challenges might be fixed by you thinking in the opposite way to the way you normally thought.

We have been taught that we are hunter-gathers; perhaps another reason we believe we are meat eaters, if you were to become a gather-hunter foraging in your own garden; you will have taken the first step. Remember my story is about the individual worlds you all live in, it all starts with you because you are the co-creator of your own world, and each individual has the innate power to change the world they live in. When each individual takes responsibility for their own actions at any given moment and begin making the changes they perceive that need to happen, will we be able to return to the garden of Eden?

Michael … Good point, I will start my veggie garden this week. If everything is constantly changing how do we learn to make changes in any given moment?

Aran … Think of an actor in a movie; the best actors play out each second in time with the film script as it unfolds. They are not thinking did I play that last scene correctly or wondering what the next scene is going to be. If they were it would show up in the end result, and the film would probably be a flop as the acting was so bad the film would have no continuity; it would be out of time. A good actor plays each scene as its meant to be played, changing the character in tune with the unfolding of the story.

A bad actor is constantly questioning and judging what was or what will be, they are in a form of conflict, they are always out of sync with the unfolding storyline they are reacting. You are all lead actors in the unfolding story of the film of your own life. Each second is a new scene that has never happened before and will never happen again, you can play a similar scene but never the same scene. When you question and judge what has already happened or what will be, you become out of sync with the unfolding story; now you are reactors and reactors are always in conflict.

You play the same scene over and over; usually in your head, hoping to get it right, life has moved on, and you are out of time.

What you see, hear, smell, taste and touch in any given moment are the real scenes you are acting in because this is the moment in time where you exist, so if what you're thinking isn't in your immediate environment you must be reacting or imagining what it should be. It is the same as when we act out somebody else's part or begin pointing out where they are going wrong and what they should be doing in order to bring the film back into harmony, you are reacting, and you will have to pay the consequences for your lack of awareness. It is time to stop the blame game, a time of forgiveness and to return to traditional community values.

It doesn't matter where you came from or where you are heading, all that truly matters is what are you doing right now in this very moment of your life. Are you acting or reacting, are you co-creating the kind of world you want to live in?

Michael … Let's take another break; I want to think about some of the things you have just mentioned, how they relate to my own personal life.

Aran … Ok that a good idea, I would like to finish by saying.

Life goes in one direction, forward, the past is called the past for a reason.

Nature does not produce waste or pollution as everything is recycled in a continuous flow called life, nature is about opposing forces working in harmony creating a pleasing and consistent whole.

So my question to you all is, as an integrated part of the nature of this planet can you learn to work in harmony free from conflict.

Can you learn to act in such a way to restore balance within your own world and in such a way that it will benefit the whole of existence?

If your answer is yes, then do it, don't just talk about it and tell others what they should be doing join me in the silent revolution.

There is no denying that each one of you knows the difference between right and wrong, after all, you point it out all the time, especially when you perceive it being done by another. You can become the change in your own world that you believe needs to happen for Unity, respect, equality, freedom and community to flourish using the higher intelligence that flows through you all as the creative process.

So as an individual taking responsibility for your own actions you really can make a difference to humanity you really can change your world.

A NEW FOUNDATION
TO BUILD UPON

Michael ... We ended the last conversation with you asking people to join the silent revolution. What do you think needs to be done for this revolution to take place?

Aran ...... The majority of people already know what's wrong with the world they live in and the changes they would like to see happen. Talking about what's wrong with the world will only keep that particular vibration in play as we have already discussed, and this is why I am calling it, the silent revolution, a time to stop talking and start acting. It is the time of action, a time for taking personal responsibility and doing what you as a unique individual knows needs to be done. It is time for humanity to grow up and become an adult, by learning to be part of the solutions and stop being a part of the problem. Once humanity remembers we truly are all one, starts acting as such and stops blaming each other for the challenges humanity as a whole has caused, can and will this change begin.

I already mentioned that each person lives in their own unique world, and all the worlds are interconnected, owing to the fact, that everything comes from the same source. Because everything is interconnected then what happens in one world affects all the others, and it is all to do with vibration. Vibration in my world represents the unspoken communication between things, the ability to communicate without words; you might call this intuition or your inner sense. Our attachment to words; the false prophets, over our senses often leads us to conflict; we may argue over the words without ever having experienced what we are arguing about. Using only one sense and ignoring the others is, according to my worldview, what I call a senseless act.

Michael ... So when we talk about what needs to happen but do nothing about it personally to bring about these changes, them we are being senseless because we are adding to the thing we want to stop.

Aran ... Yes, that's what I mean by senseless, we know what needs to be done but do nothing about it except complain that it's not happening fast enough. Complaining about these imaginary ideas is only adding to the vibration of conflict on the planet.

We are sentient beings, meaning, we are able to sense and feel things, this is our first sense, not our sixth sense as we have been told.

I sense the world around me and before thought enters the equation it is just an experience that is neither good or bad. All first sensory information is valid.

The information sensed by the body is then sent as signals to my brain where it is analysed and compared to all the other stored information from previous encounters, the valid information has now been filtered, what is left is what you imagine and believe it to be.

Michael … How does this filtering work?

Aran … The first set of filters happens because of the physical bodies limitations. We can only see certain frequencies of light and only hear certain frequencies of sound, even our sense of touch is limited to a certain frequency of temperature. There is no denying that there are other frequencies of sight, sound and temp that are present and happening all around us right this very minute even if we are not aware of them.

The amount of information that is happening in any given moment is too much for our physical body to decipher all at once. On top of this, we filter out anything that we are not focused upon, or we have no interest in.

Some scientists believe we filter out over ninth-percent and possibly up to ninety-nine percent of what is actually happening at any given moment, and this is why I say we all live in a unique world of our own choosing.

Each person filters are unique to them; we may be outside on a cold, wet and windy day, but we will each have an individual experience of that day.

We all sensed the same cold, wet and wind but our brain perceived the experience uniquely.

Thoughts in my story are a secondary sense, owing to the fact that they happen after the bodies first sense of the valid information as it happened; although we use thought for the most part as a first sense. Once the information has been sent to the brain and filtered, what really happened has already passed, so, thoughts are always based in the past of what was.

The brain then tells my body what just happened and this, in turn, creates a feeling or emotion. My body then sends out this vibration as a signal and the world responds with an experience equal to the vibration I have emitted, this is so I this body can understand if I am working with or against the source energy as a co-creator. The world, universe, god or whatever you call everything as a whole does not judge our actions, it only responds to the vibration.

Michael … Can you give me an example of this process in action, please?

Aran … When you are happy people are more likely to smile at you, when you are sad people are more likely to ignore you, this has little to do with the people and more to do with your perception of them based on your own feelings and emotions.

You see a person and relate what you see to the last encounter you had with them and then treat them accordingly.

In other words, if you think you don't like them you will filter out any good points focusing only on what you perceive their negative points to be. You are choosing one aspect of them over another and in a way are trying to separate them into what you think they are simply because you do not or will not accept who and what they are.

Michael ... Is it just with people or are all out interactions filtered?

Aran ... It happens in all our interactions, take the weather for instance, when you are happy and in a good mood, you probably don't mind getting wet from the rain. When you are sad or angry though the rain and getting wet can and often will annoy you. The rain is just rain; it didn't cause your feelings and emotions, it's what you think about what you sense that causes you to have a particular reaction. You are the cause and the effect; it is all about you and your personal relationship with the valid information you sense.

Michael ... Ok, so it is not what happens but how I react, and you're saying that reactions are based on thoughts.

Aran ... Yes, for the most part. Thought is a secondary sense, yet we have been taught to use it as our first sense ignoring our feelings and intuition and so putting our faith in the written and spoken word taking us out of the now and into the past or future. We live in the information age where knowledge has become king, knowledge on its own changes nothing.

Just knowing how to bake a cake isn't going to feed you.

Michael … Knowledge is important, though, isn't it.

Aran … Sure it is but as I just said, knowing how to bake a cake isn't going to feed you, is it. You need the know-how, the ingredients all need to be present, and you have to physically do it. Thoughts feelings and actions must all be present for the cake to manifest.

What you think, how you feel and how you are acting must all be in tune with the desired result. You could say this is a kind of recipe for manifestation.

Michael … So basically, what I put out is what I get back.

Aran … Yes, and it is all to do with vibration.

Vibrations and Frequencies are the way that energy interacts with itself, the universal language so to speak, it is the hidden meaning the secret message of the silent revolution.

Michael … Could you please give me an example of how this works?

Aran ... Let's look at communicating with your dog. Your dog doesn't really understand words as such; it is more the vibration you are expressing that it picks up on. You can shout with an angry tone at your dog that you love it and want to give it a hug, that it's a good dog and would it like some food, the dog will sense it's being attacked because of the vibration you are emitting and more than likely cower and stay away from you.

On the other hand, you can say to the dog in a calm and pleasant voice to come to you so you can beat it, that you hate it, and that you are going to do all manor of horrible things to it. In all probability, the dog will wag its tail and come running over to you. Vibration is the hidden message behind what is being said. It is more to do with what the dog senses than what it hears.

If you were to meet a person from a foreign country that didn't speak your language, you would probably have difficulty understanding them by only trying to decipher the words they spoke. There is so much more valid information you can take into consideration, their tone of voice, their body language, the repetition of certain sounds, putting all this together you can usually get a sense of what they are trying to convey.

Michael … That makes sense. I understand what you were saying; I have done some traveling myself abroad, and you are right about having a sense of what is being conveyed once you get out of your head.

It also makes sense what you said earlier about angry protesting to stop conflict only adding to the conflict. How shouting at my children to be quiet really does send them the wrong message. It's strange how you can do something over and over again without realising what it is you are actually doing. All those mixed messages I sent to my children to be quiet, all the conflict that I was responsible for, just because I wasn't paying attention to what I was actually doing in the moment.

Aran … It's not so much the verbal information that you are given; it's how you are reacting to that information that shapes your world.

There is lots of miscommunication happening because we believe in words as being the truth when in fact they are just words. Words mean what I want them to mean, what you believe they mean, or what we agree they mean. Depending on the tone of your voice a simple sentence like 'go to your room' can be a question, a statement or a command.

Written words are more easily misunderstood, and that is why I have said there is no truth in the words of this story, only possibilities. Each person listening or reading this will have a uniquely personal experience depending on their filtering system, you will only receive the information you are focused on. If you are looking for connections you may like this story and if you're not looking, you probably won't.

Michael …… Getting back to the idea that everything is interconnected, and it all comes from the same source, If you had to give this source energy a name, what would it be?

Aran … Consciousness, In my story consciousness, is the source of everything, it is the creative force behind all things. It is both the eternal and transient energy; consciousness is the soul/sole energy.

The reason for both spellings here is because as we just discussed words can have very different meanings. When either word is just spoken it carries the same vibration, only when it is written is the vibration changed, and now it's separated to express different frequencies.

Before there were any written languages people were still able to communicate and probably did so with greater accuracy as the sounds they spoke were equivalent to the vibration of the thing they were expressing. Once written words came into the equation, all sorts of communication problems arose, words like there, their, and they're. When used simply in conversation the spelling makes no difference, and you will know, for the most part, what I actually mean.

When these words are written down, they can completely change the meaning of the sentence communicated.

In this story consciousness is the 'one and only' source energy, the soul/sole energy and it communicates using vibration, not words.

We are a part of this source energy that has been manifest as physical nature, and there is no denying that nature also communicates without words. When I sense the world I live in; it is easier to recognise if I am working with the source or against it, I can also make the necessary adjustments to restore harmony in my world without the use of words.

There is a secret message in this story as I said, but, you will have to find it for yourself, because I cannot express it using words and if I did it would no longer be a secret. Going back to communicating with the dog, it wasn't the words, but the vibration that was being communicated behind the words, that was the real message.

Michael ... So by paying attention to my own vibration, I can recognise if I am working with the whole or not.

Aran ... Yes, the vibrations to pay the closest attention to would be expansion and contraction, or love and fear as they are most easily experienced in the physical body. Love being the feeling of expansion and fear the feeling of contraction. The thing is it's not about one or the other as in choosing one over the other; its more about using then to recognise which direction you are heading. Because in this story consciousness is a duality the expression of opposites working in harmony, so without love there would be no fear. Take light and dark, for instance, if there was only darkness there would be nothing to see, and if there was only light there would be nothing to see, It is the dual nature of light and dark working together harmoniously that allows us to see form. It is the same with love and fear expressed as the vibrations of expansion and contraction, without both being present there would be nothing to sense.

This I will call natural conflict as the continuous movement to and fro, the conscious vibration within all things. The reason I said conscious vibration is because they are aware of and responding to each other.

Unnatural conflict is the idea that one has power over the other, that one frequency is more important than the other, this form of conflict leads to the illusion of separation something we all sense as unnatural.

It is the acceptance of them both as aspects of the whole that creates unity or the state of forming a pleasing and consistent whole, the expression of opposites working in harmony. Its never about this or that, good or bad because both exist simultaneously. What was bad for you today may be good for you tomorrow and what is bad for you in an experience, can be good for me. So both good and bad exist simultaneously in every experience, and it is the acceptance of both as being of equal importance that will set you free from attachment to one over the other as being of more importance.

Michael ... Earlier on you mentioned how it is my thoughts that allow me to perceive a person a particular way, having either a positive or negative reaction towards them. I have chosen one aspect of them over the other causing a form of separation, a contraction, and this is all based on my thought process. So how do I restore harmony?

Aran ... There is a common ground for everything, race, creed, colour, social, political and religious beliefs when you are able to share this common ground you create harmony instead of conflict.

The story that I want to tell is of the game of life played between I the body and myself the consciousness, a game that is best played with unconditional unity and played just for the experience of playing.

If everything truly is connected then when or if one part wins another part loses and everything suffers as a consequence.

Michael … How do we find this common ground you just mentioned.

Aran … Take religion, for example; no religious person disagrees that there is a God, only to what is should be called and how it should be worshiped.

You all know deep down inside what is meant if I say the word God, but because you call it something else we may disagree on what God is.

These differences over the names used cause the sense of separation, as in, a Muslim is not a Jew, and a Christian is neither a Jew or a Muslim.

This kind of belief that one idea is more important than another causes them to think they are separate from each other, which as we have seen can lead to some serious conflict both verbal and physical.

On the other hand, the similarity is, they are all religious people who believe in God. They are all conceived and born the same way, they have the same internal organs, they all need food, water, fresh air, shelter and companionship for their ongoing and healthy survival, and they all rely on nature to supply these needs.

This way of thinking can cause a sense of unity, With the use of unconditional unity I can hold to my belief and allow others to hold to theirs. To me, this is a true compromise, we both get what we want without either of us giving anything up, this is what I mean by the middle path or common ground. I have found it is more beneficial to look for the similarities and how through the sharing of our differences with respect to the others beliefs and understanding, we can learn to recognise those similarities that were always present but perhaps filtered out.

Michael … I've heard a lot of these ideas mentioned before so whats so different about your story?

Aran … I am not trying to teach you anything or change you in any way as I have already mentioned, that isn't my job, I am just telling a story.

Most of what I say you may have heard before its common knowledge, it is not so much about the story or the common knowledge it is more about what you do with the knowledge and what you do with it, is up to you.

Knowing something doesn't necessarily change anything, knowledge in my story is just the accumulation of information, whereas understanding comes from the use of that information. Memorizing a recipe and then being able to recite it is not the same as making the dish.

Knowledge feeds the mind; understanding feeds the whole body.

There is a quote from Mahatma Gandhi, "Be the change you want to see in the world ". What if all these individual worlds are connected and what you do in your world actually does affect the whole. What if your vibration was the energy that tipped the scale towards total harmony and unity for and in all worlds, don't you owe it to yourself and everyone else to at least try.

Michael … Do you seriously think one person can make such a difference when it comes to changing the world?

Aran … If everything truly is interconnected as science and philosophy are implying, then, yes I do. Think of the many worlds theory from the point of view of a meditation circle. In a meditation circle, regardless of the number of people in it, you may be guided to a beach or a forest, and although you all hear the same words from the person guiding the meditation, you all have our own unique experience and no two people create the same imaginary place. This doesn't just happen when we meditate, we are all offered the same information from the world around us and just like in the meditation circle, we all perceive the world in our own unique way. This is how I co-create my world, and because everything is interconnected what I co-create effects the whole.

Michael … Ok, so one person can make a difference.

Aran … As I mentioned earlier, I call this the many worlds theory and my story is simply about what it means to be me in my world. I recognise that when I vibrate happiness the whole of creation benefits and when I vibrate sadness everything suffers, this is the innate power I have within me to change the world. When I don't take personal responsibility for my actions and their consequences, and how I perceive them in my world, I am more likely to blame someone or something perceived as outside or separate from me as the cause of my pain and suffering. This experience can only manifest for me when I have forgotten that everything actually means everything, I cannot add or subtract from everything simply because it has nowhere to come from or go to except itself. If I am trying to separate from the whole, I am attempting to create a reality where more or less is required for unconditional unity to exist.

Going back to the meditation circle it is not what you hear that creates your imaginary world, its what you think about what you heard. Remember in this story if I feel it or think it, then it belongs to me, it is my responsibility. It is how I am responding to the valid information that I was offered. Just like leading a meditation circle, I may not be responsible for how others feel, but I am responsible for the vibration I emit.

Michael… I have heard the word responsibility used that way before, as being my ability to respond. What did you mean by, if I think it, or feel it, it is a part of me? What about how others make me feel. Hold that answer; I just realised what I said, it is not what others do is it, its how I respond, that's what you were saying wasn't it.

Aran … Yes, I was. To answer your question, I cannot think of something without the vibration of what I am thinking already being present within me, and I cannot feel something without that vibration being present within me either. So if I think it or feel it, it is already a part of me, it is now my responsibility if I don't want to feel this vibration. All that I am asking is that you try some of the ideas that are being expressed here, especially those ideas that make you go, Aha, right I get it. Then and only then will you understand the secret concepts behind the words in the story for yourself, only then can and will you join the silent revolution.

Michael … I like what you were saying about the meditation circle and how we all imagine our own unique experience even though we were all given the same information, I can even recognise how this process works in my daily life, and how we each create our own unique life experience.

So my next question is why do I create both good and bad experiences for myself, what is the benefit of a bad experience?

Aran … The possibility of both good and bad are present in every experience whether you are aware of this fact or not, they are merely the expressions of opposites working in harmony. Without one, the other would cease to exist. You are not the creator of the good and bad experience because they both already exist you are however the experiencer. You do however have the ability to focus on either frequency independently, allowing you to be a co-creator in the total atmosphere of existence, and you do this by focusing on one or the other. You have been given the ability to be a co-creator, to work with the source energy by moving along the middle ground accepting both sides as valid information and also work against it by choosing one side over the other. Only as a physical body is consciousness able to act this way.

The human body is a transceiver; a device that can both transmit and receive communications. Think of yourself as a mobile radio station that has been manifest for the soul purpose of receiving and transmitting information from and to the source energy of consciousness, so consciousness can experience the endless possibilities of frequency within itself. It doesn't matter what any other station is receiving and transmitting; it isn't your job to get involved in the running of another station unless that station has asked for help. Each of you as a mobile station has been given autonomy, the right and condition of self-government, to play out any frequency it personally chooses and it does this with the use of the focus of the mind manager.

The mind managers job is to facilitate the smooth running of the station it is in charge of, so the signals can be received and transmitted with the highest clarity free from any interference. This job can only be achieved when the mind manager gives its undivided attention to its own station and the signal it is emitting.

When you only pay attention to the job that you have been manifest to do, to receive and transmit information from and to the source without judgement and free from any interference then you are being enough and are worthy of your purpose as a co-creator. Your payment for doing your job is a harmonious relationship with the whole. When your judgemental mind manager interferes with the clarity of the signal from the source, in the futile hope of creating a frequency that is separate from the one received, the signal you are emitting will be out of harmony with the original signal. The foundation of your station; your physical body, starts to shake and crumble to let you know; you are acting out of sync.

Michael ... When I feel out of sync it becomes my responsibility, as the mind manager, to do something about it then.

Aran ... Yes, When the mind manager thinks it knows better that the source signal what should be transmitted it is out of sync. What you sense is the valid signal received from the source, what you thought about what you sensed was the mind manager judging the signal and what you emitted was your response. The only thing that you need to change for harmony to be restored in any interaction is the mind managers reaction.

So once again it is not the information you are given, its what you think about that information that has the biggest impact upon you.

Thinking is both a blessing and a curse as both good and bad thoughts cause a sense of separation.

The secret to this story isn't in the words; it is the hidden meaning behind the words that can only be found by acting out this information with unconditional unity. It is about the acceptance of both sides as being of equal importance as the opposing forces that create and maintain a consistent and pleasing whole. It isn't even my secret, it is more a secret message from the source, some have called it enlightenment, to be the light and as the light nothing is or can be hidden from you anymore. It is a state of being that can only be experienced to be understood, I cannot tell you or show you this state of being, but you will know when you are there.

When you become the one in the all, there is no longer any need for words; questions cease to exist and all that remains is the experience.

CONSCIOUSNESS AND EVERYTHING

Michael ... You mentioned earlier that in your world the source of everything is consciousness, that it is the infinite and finite, the one and the all, so can we talk about this conscious everything and what it means to you. Can you give an example of how it is one thing and everything at the same time, please?

Aran ... I will start by trying to explain what I mean by everything. The word everything means, all things, the whole, this implies you cannot add or subtract from everything because it has nowhere else to come from or go to except itself. Everything is much more than the word, it is the source of all that is, was and ever will be, it is the ever-changing undivided complete conscious whole. The biggest challenge in telling this story is trying to explain everything using physical words. Everything as the source is both physical and the non-physical, and although I can use words to express the physical aspects, there are no words that I can use to express truly the non-physical other than to say it is Everything.

Water can be a good example of one thing and many things at the same time, so let's look at it using the example of water. Try and imagine that everything is the ocean of consciousness, like an ocean it is one thing and many things at the same time; the all and the nothing. When you look at an ocean, you see one whole thing, a body of water, but when you look more closely you realise, this ocean, this whole body of water is made up of innumerable molecules of water. In 1 millilitre of water, there are approximately 3.34 X 10 ^ 23; That's 3.34 X 100000000000000000000000 molecules. Each molecule is an individual drop of water and all the molecules together are also water. The number of molecules in all the water on the planet is beyond most people's comprehension, so to the number of things within everything. Water is one thing and many things at the same time; I hope that makes sense?

Michael ... I think so; you are saying there are the individual molecules that are basically water, then, there are the innumerable molecules together as a whole that are basically water. It's basically the same explanation with consciousness; there is consciousness as a complete whole that is made up of individual drops of consciousness.

Aran ... Yes, the parts and the whole are one and the same, and in the same way, what we call physical and non-physical are one and the same thing also, because everything comes from the same source that is interconnected, interactive and works as a complete whole. The individual parts cannot be divided from the whole.

The all affects the one, and the one affects the all simultaneously, because everything is, was and always will contain everything. Words as I mentioned cause a kind of separation and an example of this would be to look at water again and the amount of descriptive words we use to express all the qualities of and within water. Fog, dew, snow, sleet, hail, vapour, steam, Ocean, sea, river, stream, brook, lake, puddle, ice, Etc. Any of these descriptive words that you use are just expressions of a quality or an aspect of water. Being an aspect doesn't mean it is separate from it because at the fundamental level they are all descriptions of water.

Modern and ancient science as well as philosophy propose that everything is interconnected and interactive, so to me this implies that everything is conscious, as the word conscious means, aware of and responsive to its environment. There is the thing that is aware and the thing it is responsive to, so this implies everything as a whole is a conscious duality. It is a duality simply because there are two parts, aspects or qualities to it, the thing that is aware and the thing it is responsive to, everything as a whole is having a conscious relationship with and within itself.

Michael … Wait a minute, are you saying that existence is simply consciousness having a relationship with itself?

Aran … Yes, that the best explanation that I can give. You as a part of this consciousness are part of this relationship, that's why I have said that what you do effect's the whole, you are not, never have, or will be separate from the whole. The whole is conscious of itself as a whole, and the individual parts are conscious of themselves as a whole part, but there is only one consciousness, and there is only one relationship.

When you look up the origin of the word individual in a dictionary it means, not divisible, or cannot be divided. The part that is aware and the part it is responsive to; are not separate from each other simply because the whole cannot be added to or subtracted from, it cannot be divided, and that is why I say that separation is just a thought. As a unique individual being you are not, never have or will be separate from the whole either. You are affected and have an effect on each other simultaneously this is the conscious relationship.

Science and philosophy also propose that everything; what I will now refer to as consciousness, can be expressed as energy that cannot be created or destroyed, only transferred or transformed into another form of energy, this implies that the consciousness of everything is eternal.

This conscious relationship is eternal; without beginning or end, and you as an aspect of this relationship are also eternal. So, there is this eternal conscious energy that is constantly interacting with itself transforming and transferring within itself as both the transient and eternal energies, what we have come to call the physical and non-physical aspects of life.

This eternal conscious energy is dual in nature, and the unconditional acceptance of this duality of everything is the key to unity.

Michael … Are you saying that duality and unity are in a sense one and the same thing?

Aran … The parts and the whole are one and the same yes. As I just mentioned there is always a challenge using words when trying to explain the non-physical aspects of everything, simply because the non-physical has no words in it. Think of it this way before the advent of telescopes and microscopes the known universe was just what could be seen and understood with the naked eyes, so there was the somethings that could be seen and the nothings that couldn't. Now with space telescopes and electron microscopes we have realised where there was once nothing, there is now something. I wonder if you understand though that nothing only becomes something once you name it. It still existed before it had a name and even though you couldn't physically see, it was still there.

The more powerful the electron microscopes become; approx. Twenty-million times more powerful than the naked eye, the more similar the things seem to become and just like the molecules of water are all similar but still individual, the parts of the whole are similar but individual.

Everything is an ocean of conscious energy that contains innumerable conscious things that are constantly transferring and transforming within the whole; nothing can happen outside the whole because everything is, was, and always will be contained within itself. Everything cannot be added to or subtracted from because there is only one source energy from which all things are manifest. Just like snow, ice, steam, Etc., which in a sense are the transient energies of water, that came from water and then return to water. So plants, trees, animals, birds, fish, humans, planets, solar systems, all physical forms in-fact are transient energy, they all come into existence and go out of existence, but they all come from and return to the same source. Everything is both the something and the nothing at the same time, it is the physical and non-physical, it is not one or the other, it is both simultaneously. As I just said, before something has a name it is nothing, then it is given a name and now it's a something, with or without a name it still existed as energy, it was still a thing within everything.

Michael … If I understand you correctly, you're saying that everything has a dual quality, and this dual quality as the source energy is what you are calling consciousness.

Aran … Yes, consciousness is the creative force behind all manifestations, anything can only come from everything, the seen and the unseen are the expressions of the conscious relationship within the whole. Without one, the other would cease to exist, and there would be nothing.

Michael … OK, that makes sense. Getting back to the idea that everything actually means every-thing where do we come into this story

Aran… We are already in it and have been all the time, we are pure consciousness, we are everything. Even though consciousness cannot be separated from itself, as a physical form it can express one aspect of its duality over the other for short periods of time, this form of energy is short-lived because it is transient. The physical body is a form of transient energy so it to is short lived, but the consciousness from which it was manifest is eternal. I am the consciousness, not the body.

Michael ... I think that I am beginning to understand, you are saying that consciousness has two qualities, eternal, and transient, these are then expressed as the non-physical and the physical respectively. Also that these qualities are intrinsically linked to each other in the relationship it is having with itself.

Aran ... Yes, Each thing within everything is manifest from pure conscious energy and where it came from, where it is going and where it exist right now are all one and the same place. The individual parts of the whole cannot be divided from the whole.

Michael ... Then anything and everything that happens is a conscious creation whether we experience it as good or bad?

Aran ... To me, yes it is. There isn't good or bad though because this implies two separate sources, there is only good and bad, and both exist simultaneously. What we call life and death are not separate from each other either, they are merely the transformation of energy from one form into another and back again, the conscious dance of everything in the ever changing innumerable possibilities of existence.

Michael ... If everything is consciousness that cannot be separated from itself, how do you explain the human physical body that experiences separation from the whole, what is the reason for physical life?

Aran … Think about it this way; the eternal consciousness has manifested within itself an instrument for a scientific experiment that can express the duality of consciousness as the individual frequencies of the vibration.

It is only able to experience duality this way as a physical instrument, the transient human body. Only as a transient physical energy can the human body experience transient energies that are expressed as the individual frequencies within duality.

This experience is transient and always short lived because only expressing one quality at a time it is out of harmony with itself as unity.

Separation isn't a reality; it is merely a thought process used for gaining an understanding of duality.

Michael …So you are saying that creation is so consciousness can understand its duality?

Aran … Basically yes, Consciousness is looking into itself and its dual action of frequency within the vibration of all things; this is how consciousness learns in and of itself as so evolves. The first thing you need to understand here is that it is the physical bodies that are having this conversation. Only as a physical body does consciousness use words to communicate. Only as a physical body is there an idea of separation.

Consciousness is never separate from itself and does not use words to communicate as words cause a kind of separation.

Pure consciousness communicates through vibration. If I say, it is this, I am also expressing, it is not that. Separation is a construct of the scientific instrument of the body, and as I've already said without this ability to compare, the conscious manifestation of the body would not be able to learn about the individual qualities of duality and act as a co-creator.

Michael ... So consciousness is the creative force behind all things and is eternal, the physical body that is transient and, therefore, can only be a co-creator.

Aran ... That's right, and although each body is uniquely individual it is never separate from the whole, it is however only transient this is why it is consciousness that is the creator, and the physical body is only a co-creator.

Michael ... Once I get my judgemental mind manager out of the way, it all makes perfect sense. What are these qualities of duality and how can we as the body learn to recognise them?

Aran ... These qualities are physically expressed as expansion and contraction, the coming together and the moving apart without ever being separate from each other. You can feel them when you breathe as they work in harmony with each other, try only breathing in or out and you will soon realise the importance of duality. The physical body is an instrument created to experiences the qualities when it does so holistically it accepts this movement of to and fro as of equal importance and has a harmonious relationship within the whole of creation. These dual qualities might be experienced as good and bad, light and dark, right and wrong, etc. Do you recognise it is only when the body chooses one quality over the other as being of more importance that conflict arises, simply because it is trying to create a reality where only one quality exists?

Conflict only arises when both the qualities of duality are not present.

Michael … Let's just see if I've got this right. This consciousness has manifested within itself a physical body for the sole purpose of understanding the process of creation, and only as a physical body is it able to understand if it is working for or against itself.

Aran … Yes, consciousness is having a relationship with itself.

I would like to talk about where the idea of separation came from and how you might be able to free yourself from the illusion of that idea.

How you can recognise your connection to everything once again and sense the wholeness that you are manifest from, by using some of the techniques that have helped me remember who and what I truly am.

Each one of us lives in a unique world of our own choosing, so, if you recognise something, in my world, that might make a difference in your world, that not only benefits you but the whole of creation, it is your responsibility to make it happen. Don't wait for a saviour; you are the most powerful person you will ever meet, because you and you alone have the power to change the world in which you live.

Michael ... Before we finish for the day Aran, I would like to talk quickly about the idea of you being a walk-in as I believe this has something to do with you being able to recognise the connection between the eternal and the transient energies of consciousness.

Aran ... Ok, I came into this world in much the same way as everything else, with a transition from one energy into another. Birth and death are only the beginning and ending of the physical form but the life force, or consciousness the non-physical aspect of us all is eternal. The only difference between how I entered into this body as a walk-in and how you entered into yours. As a walk-in, I am not conditioned in the same way that this is my body. I took over an empty vessel that was already formed and so didn't have to go through the birthing process, a process that binds and conditions the consciousness to the physical body. I remember I am the consciousness, not the body. I am not conditioned to the body as who I am, simply because I wasn't born as a body, this doesn't make me or any other walk-in special, we still have the same challenges of being in a physical being like everyone else.

If I were to think of who I am as special, then in a sense, I am saying I'm more important than other things or other people, this is an illusion of being separate and this would attach me to the transient consciousness of the physical body as being who I am. No one thing in everything is more or less important than any other thing in everything, as a walk-in I understand this, but, it doesn't make me special.

We are all manifest from the same source as unique individuals to have a unique individual experience within this conscious relationship called life.

In this story nobody knows more or less than anybody else, we all just know different things and in the sharing of our differences using unconditional unity as the foundation of our relationships, we can and will end all unnatural conflict on this plane of existence.

Michael … Thank you Aran, That last statement is a hopeful statement to finish with today.

THE BODY AND DUALITY

Michael … We were talking about the connection of everything as a whole and the quality of duality. So I'm wondering if we can look into what it means to be just a physical body in this reality now, you imply that the physical body has been manifest as an instrument of consciousness to understand better the relationship with itself.

Aran … Ok, Michael That would be a good idea as I was going to ask if we could focus more on the physical side of life, as that is what the majority of this story is about. What it means to be a physical body in this conscious relationship between I and myself. Let's look at duality a little more closely as it exists in my story and then we will look into the physical body and how it fits into duality.

As I have already stated, duality is the expression of opposites working in harmony; these opposites are not separate from each other in the same way that day and night are not separate from each other. Day and night are a continuation of each other; it is only through the use of the words; day and night, that the idea of separation arises. We need to look at duality from a holistic point of view, not as this or that, but, as this and that, and recognise how all the parts fit together.

The Un-manifested and the manifested are the two primary qualities of conscious duality.

Michael ... So oneness or unity in your story has two parts that are inseparable from each other, meaning oneness and duality are one and the same?

Aran ... Yes, I know that is a bit of a contradiction but so was the idea of everything being one thing and everything at the same time. As I just mentioned day and night are a continuation of each other, they are not really separate from each other; it is only the use of the words day and night that create the belief they are separate.

Michael ...If words have created the belief of separation, as a state of existence, is it possible to experience life as a human being without this belief entering into our daily existence and experiences?

Aran ... I have experienced it that way, so, I would have to say yes it is possible. Words are merely the expression of the different frequencies within the energy of everything. It is a fact that words have been given far more power than they deserve, and I for one see how this has lead to the parts being of more importance than the whole. When you shine a white light through a prism, that light is broken down into the seven colours of the visible spectrum, all the colours came from the same source and would not exist without the source energy being present. As soon as those colours have been given a name they are now expressed as being separate from that source and each other, some colours are even expressed as being more important and powerful than the source from which they were created. I do not deny that different colours have different frequencies but the very idea that one colour is more important than any other colour or the source from which it came only serves the idea separation as a reality. The one as the source and the many as the colours cannot be separated from each other; they are the individual parts that make up the whole.

Consciousness is the source, and the colours are the physical representation of that source energy.

Michael … I understand what you are saying but the colours are more than one thing so how does this fit with your idea of duality.

Aran … There is the source as the white light and the colours as the physical expression of the source light. The non-physical as the source, and the physical as the colours represent the dual nature of consciousness. All the colours are not separate from each other simply because everything in the physical and non-physical is interconnected; it is only the use of words that give the idea of separation. I understand this can be challenging to get your head around; I also know that somewhere deep inside of you when you stop questioning you recognise what I am talking about.

Michael … I must admit I am kind of in two minds over this. Is this the expression of duality within me, the coming together and the moving apart, the non-verbal understanding of wholeness and the verbal idea of separation, so to speak?

Aran … Perhaps that is one way of looking at it. There is a state of being called enlightenment when everything is experienced as one. To me enlightenment means to be the light, to be the eternal source, not the transient physical representation of it. It is a fact that even in the darkest of places one tiny amount of light can dispel the darkness, so to be the light implies it is the state when nothing can or is hidden. To be the light, I am one with the source and its infinite frequencies; I am the part and the whole. What I am and what I perceive are one and the same, there is no division once you become the light.

There are no questions or answers there is only the pure relationship of consciousness between the one and the all.

Michael … Enlightenment is another of these secrets you have mentioned that you must find for yourself, it is a state of being that is beyond words so it can only be implied at, but I like your explanation of it.

Aran … I cannot tell you what enlightenment is like, but you will know when you get there.

Michael … That makes sense, are you enlightened Aran?

Aran … If I were to answer yes, then you would know that I'm not.

Michael ... Getting back to colour as all being of equal importance, some people use colour therapy and it seems to have a beneficial effect on the human body. So, how would you account for the use of colour in this way, especially as one colour may be used above all the others in a session and you said that no one colour is of more importance than another?

Aran ... To have balance within an individual body or the whole, then all the parts need to be present. When the physical body is out of balance, it has filtered out certain frequencies as it tries to create an existence separate from the whole.

When the physical body uses an excess or decrease of any frequency, it becomes out of balance and this is felt as dis-ease in any of its myriad forms of expression; mental, emotional, physical and spiritual. Any form of therapy, colour or otherwise, is used to restore harmony between the parts and the whole caused by the excess or decrease. All the frequencies need to be present for the connection to the source to be harmonious; this is why I am saying that no one colour is more important than any other colour. The colour therapist is restoring balance in the instrument because unless all the colours are present in equal quantities, the physical instrument of the manifest body is out of tune with the source. Once all the colours or frequencies are present the body is once able to reconnect to the source.

Think of the prism again, the white light and the seven colours are in perfect balance, if you were to take away one colour would that still be the case?

Michael …Ok, I see where you are going with that.

Aran … When the body thinks it knows better that the source what life should be, it is trying to be the creator, it is trying to create a reality where not all the colours exist; it is trying to separate duality, This will inevitably lead to conflict with what is and disease. When the body realises it is merely just an instrument of consciousness and an integrated part of the whole and acts accordingly working with the whole to be a co-creator of balance it is working in harmony.

We were manifest to be co-creators working with the whole, not creators working against the whole.

Michael … That make sense to me at least, on so many levels, especially when you said that disease is the lack or excess of a particular frequency within my body. Too much or too little of anything can have an adverse effect, so you really can have too much of a good thing. How can we learn to work with the whole and not against it?

Aran … First, you will have to remember it is all one complete whole, then and only then will you sense and understand it for what it actually is. That understanding of unity or wholeness is something you can only realise for yourselves; once you have experienced it, there is no going back.

As I mentioned nobody can teach you to be enlightened they can only point you in the right direction, it is a journey that must be taken alone. I have seen courses on the internet and billboards offering classes in enlightenment as if it is something you can buy with money, a commodity. As a unique individual, you cannot follow somebody else's path to enlightenment because it is a state beyond words, it is a secret place you have to find for yourself. If I or anybody could simply tell you what to do, then surely the world would be full of enlightened people.

Michael … If only enlightenment was that easy? Can you explain, please, what you mean about the difference between knowledge and understanding?

Aran … I can teach you my knowledge, but I can't teach you my understanding.

Just think about meditation for a moment, I can teach you everything I know about meditation, posture, breathing, relaxation techniques, but I can't teach you what I experience during a deep meditative state because words will never do it justice. The understanding comes in the silence. Knowledge can be shared orally whereas the understanding of what you experience is truly personal and unique.

Michael … So when you say the secret behind the words or the knowledge then, this is what you mean.

Aran … By putting knowledge into practice, the true secrets of life can be experienced first hand. Knowledge comes through information and understanding comes through physical experience of knowledge; in this story at least.

Michael … I see what you are getting at here, I have read many self-help books and have accumulated a vast amount of knowledge, but little has changed in my life apart from the fact that I think I now know what to do and often tell other people what I think they should do. What you are saying is that unless I put into practice what I know is the right choice for me, I will never reach an understanding. So I can buy knowledge but not understanding because understanding is always a unique and secret experience.

Aran ... Yes pretty much, and once you understand something, it is far better to walk your talk than just to talk about it.

Michael ... So is enlightenment the ability to understand my connection to everything physically and non-physically without allowing a thought to enter into the equation. In other words to just be. A tree is a tree it interacts with its environment, but it doesn't try to be anything other than a tree.

Aran ... I see what you mean, So you are asking is it possible for the body to act just as a body, an integrated part of the whole and not try to be anything other than what it is.

Michael ... Yes, can the body interact with its environment without causing any form of conflict or separation?

Aran ... If you were manifested by consciousness as a scientific experiment to understand truly the relationship between all things, then perhaps, you need to act like a scientist and check it out for yourself. After all, you have been given the equipment to do the experiment with. Start with something simple like, how much of your daily life is spent thinking about what was, the past, and what might be, the future.

Look at your watch or the clock; each second is a one off unique moment in time, when you act out each moment, in the moment, you are in time.

When you are thinking about the past or future event you are out of time.

This unique gift from source as the gift of now is simply to be experienced not questioned.

Michael … There has been a lot written lately about being in the present moment, what advice can you offer to help understand what being in the moment means?

Aran … Try to think about it this way for a moment. There is only one of everything, but they are all connected and interactive, Each second of the day, each moment in time is an individually unique experience that is linked together as what we call time. Do you realise that each moment only happens once, you can experience something similar but never the same thing, so once you are able to experience every moment, every second as if for the first time then I believe you will be in the moment? Music is a good example because it is made up of individual notes played one after the other, which are similar to moments that happen one after the other. When you hear a new piece of music for the first time, you have to let go of the past, as the last note, pay attention to the note being played, the present, without any thought of what the next note will be, the future. It is the repetition of this action that brings harmony to the experience of listening to music.

Michael ... So hearing music is a metaphor of how to experience life then, how to be in the moment?

Aran ... It can be yes, because when you can accept everything that you perceive in any given moment as part of the complete melody of life without conflict, you are acting harmoniously with the whole. Every vibration in the universe is a part of the melody of life, all the individual parts make up the whole, nothing can be added or subtracted because everything comes from the same source. Being in the moment is the innate ability to accept everything as it is; without any conflict being present.

Michael ... It sounds so much easier than it is to do.

Aran ... As I said, you have the equipment, do the experiment yourself and you might come to the understanding you are looking for. All information is valid because it is based on what actually is. All things communicate using vibration; this is how information is passed between things. What we call our senses sight, sound, taste, touch and smell, are nothing more that the different frequencies within the energy vibration itself that are sensed by your body, different ways to communicate the same information by breaking it down into smaller chunks to aid you in the assimilation of the information. All information is valid as it is actually supporting the intended point or claim, there is no right or wrong information there is only the communication of information between the transmitter and receiver. The body is a scientific instrument that has the ability to tune into any frequency that is expressed within the whole and is able to do this simply to learn of the endless vibrations within the source of all things and transmit them back to source.

Michael … Can we look at how I can use my body as the instrument in this science experiment, please, as I feel this could be useful in gaining an understanding?

Aran … You, or more to the point your body, is like an instrument in the orchestra of creation and each one of you plays a unique vibration that you and you alone are responsible for, keeping your instrument in tune is your only responsibility.

To understand that you are an instrument in this orchestra means that you and you alone are responsible for any vibration that is emitted by your body and that this is all that you can be responsible for, the effect of which you are the cause.

When the orchestra is sensed as being out of tune, it can only be the scientific instrument of your body that is out of tune, not the whole orchestra. So trying to change anything but your own instrument only puts you more out of tune with the orchestra. Once you understood that it is only your own instrument that is out of tune and that this is within your power to change, then it becomes your responsibility.

When the instrument of the body is happy and in-tune with the orchestra, it hums to its self, whistle tunes and dances around with joy as it is moving closely and in tune with the rhythm of life.

When it is out of tune, it grunts, huffs and bangs around to its own tune that after a while no one wants to hear any more.

Michael ... I play an instrument, in fact, I play the guitar and the piano, so this concept of being in-tune and out of tune makes sense to me.

I also now recognise how it is only humans that think the world they live in is out of balance when in fact it is we who are out of balance with the world. Its even starting to make sense about my ability to be a co-creator, and how I can actually change my world for the betterment of the whole. Using the instrument in the orchestra idea, if I am in tune or out of tune, it makes a big difference to the whole orchestra.

Aran ... That is good to hear Michael, It really is an individual life, and I hope you are beginning to sense how powerful you are, and your ability to bring about the changes needed to restore harmony within the whole.

When you are able to sense the melody of life for what it truly is; unique, fleeting moments one after another, something magical starts to happen.

I would like us to look at the physical body and its connection to nature now. Each body is intrinsically linked to the planet and cannot survive without this connection, as a human being you are only able to grow with the help of mother earth. The water you drink, the air you breathe, and the food you eat, are all products of the earth and whatever you breathe, eat, and drink, becomes the energy that allows the cells to multiply and enable the body to grow. It is the same process for both plants and animals; you truly are a part of nature. There are and have been many cultures going back over the centuries that express this nature as mother earth and father sky, and I for one don't think its just a coincidence. Together they are the forces of your garden home that supplies all your basic needs.

A need to me, at least, is something that is essential, the basic needs of a human being, a plant or an animal are food, water, fresh air, a safe environment to rest and evolve and companionship.

If you are listening or reading this, then there is no denying that all of your basic needs have been supplied from the moment of your conception up until this very moment in time; as we have already discussed.

Michael … What about the starving people, the ones that barely have enough to eat.

Aran … Remember we are talking about the body just as a body and its connection to nature here, without the ability to judge or think separately. The point I am trying to get at, is, that if you are alive right now, them somehow all your essential needs have been supplied up to this very moment in time. All that matters is that somehow they were supplied.

You may have known hunger in your lifetime and been thirsty and lonely, but the facts are, you have had enough food and water for you continued survival up to this moment in time. Your basic needs have been met.

Michael … If we have everything that we need to survive, how come some bodies die before their time, why do some have so little and some have so much more.

Aran … That way of thinking is using judgement and comparison again and for now, we are talking about the body just being a body without these abilities. I know this can be difficult, but try to think about it as if I was telling you what it is like on another planet, where money and things have nothing to do with success. Where greed, separation and a sense of mine don't exist, and where people are just a part of nature just the same as trees. Imagine a place where everything has an equal share, where nobody takes more than is required for their daily needs and requirements.

A planet where sustainability and cooperation are the norms. Imagine a world without thinking and reasoning humans and there is no denying the world would be in a much better state than it is. For all the knowledge have we amassed, are we really co-creating a better world for our children?

Michael … When you explain it that way I see what you're hinting at, if human beings weren't present on this earth I accept the fact that it would in all probability be in a far better state that it is at this present moment in time.

Aran … Getting back to your question of why some have more or less than others, and why some die before others, the answers to that are in the very nature that surrounds us. You can plant similar seeds in similar ground, supply them with the similar amount of water and nutrients and they will still have a unique life cycle; some may fade quickly, and some outlive all the others. It is the same for your physical bodies, two people can live very similar lives, similar food, water, shelter and fresh air, yet they will have their own unique life span. What we call birth and death are merely the coming and going of energy from the non-physical to the physical form and back to the non-physical in the never-ending cycle of life, the transference and the transformation from one thing to another thing. Some cycles like the cells of a body last a very short period, whereas, celestial bodies last much longer, even the universe as we know it goes through stages of physical and non-physical existence.

When one cycle ends, and another begins, as everything transfers and transforms into the next thing in this never ending existence.

I think it's vital to remember that each physical body is unique, that there is only one of everything. Let us look at the uniqueness of life. No two trees are identical in fact no two leaves on those trees are identical, everything in creation is a unique manifestation that expresses the endless vibrational possibilities that are present within the eternal soul consciousness. Each grain of sand, each snowflake, each plant, each leaf on each tree, each insect, fish and each person including what we call identical twins, are all unique individual manifestations of consciousness. They are not separate from it because everything is sourced from the same consciousness, but they are individual manifestations here for a unique experience.

Michael … I never thought about it that way before, So each and everything is here for a unique experience, and that's why you are saying that this is just your story about what it means to be you in your world.

Aran … Yes, that right, I don't know what it means to be you, and if I try, I have to use judgement and comparison. That's why my story really is about my unique take on life, what it means to be me in my world and to recognise if I am co-creating a harmonious relationship within the whole or not. As an individually unique instrument in the symphony of life, is it possible for me to express my vibrations unconditionally, and recognise the experience and the experiencer are one and the same?

Michael … Now that sounds like challenge if I ever heard one.

Aran … Take it up, what do you have to lose. Duality, as I have said in my world, is the expression of opposites working in harmony, so there isn't this or that, but there is, this and that. In my story life is a never ending cycle, just like everything as a whole, it is without beginning or end. Life and death are not the beginning and the end they are just the transformation of energy from one thing to another.

Think of a tree or a plant, an animal or any living thing for a moment and recognise how all living things are a part of this cycle of life, including you.

There is no escaping the fact that you as this body are an integrated part of nature and in truth are no more or less important than any other part of nature. As just a body without judgement or comparison, your soul purpose is simply to experience and just as a tree doesn't try to be anything other that what it is, so you too are simply here to experience and accept what is, for what it is. A unique one-off experience in the endless possibilities of existence.

Michael … So what happened to make us believe we are separate from nature, that we are above it and of more importance.

Aran … Conscious evolution, consciousness evolves in and of itself, and it has manifested all these unique individual bodies so it can experience all of its possibilities. The more physical bodies it has, the more unique experiences it can have simultaneously and so evolution speeds up. This is perhaps why the human population is at an all-time high. Our physical bodies are the next step in conscious evolution.

The earth has been evolving as an aspect of consciousness for millennia and plants, and animals had been part of the evolutionary process long before human beings came into being. As far as we know humans are the first species to question their existence, this is part of the evolutionary process because the human body was manifest for and with the capability to understand the process of manifestation. So consciousness can learn if it is co-creating harmoniously with itself or not.

Michael ... So it is not me this body that is evolving, its consciousness as a whole that is evolving through the use of this body.

Aran ... Yes, so stop thinking you are of more importance than you actually are. I know this can be difficult to get your head around, but there really isn't my consciousness and your consciousness there is only consciousness. If and when your body evolves it can only do so because it is part of the whole, it cannot evolve separately; separation is not a reality it is an illusion caused by the idea that the parts are of more importance than the whole. It's ok to think you are special as the one off unique individual you were manifest to be. It's not Ok to think you are more special than any of the other innumerable unique individuals that are alive at this very moment in time. Whether you are a street sweeper or a corporate high flier makes little difference, this elitist attitude regardless of your station in life that you are somehow of more importance than anything or anybody else in existence is a lack of your true understanding.

How dare you think you are more important than anybody else and life itself.

Michael ... How is it that the body then that is a part of everything has ended up believing it is separate and more important than it actually is.

Aran … OK, so let us look at the duality of the body again. There is I the eternal soul conscious energy, and then there is I the physical body the transient energy, remember in this part of the story we are looking at the conscious duality of everything. I will use the words body and soul to explain your dual nature as these seem to be words and concepts that most people understand.

Soul is the eternal conscious essence; it does not need a body to survive.

You do not have a soul, you are conscious soul energy, and as such are always connected to everything, simply because everything is energy.

You cannot be separate from the whole, where you as soul energy came from, where you are going and where you are right now, are all one and the same space, this is your true state of being, pure eternal and everlasting conscious soul energy.

Think of the body as an instrument created by consciousness, the eternal soul energy, for a science experiment to understand the properties of its own duality and the creation process. The body is able to act holistically characterised by the belief that the parts of something are intimately interconnected and explicable only by reference to the whole.

It is also able to act from an atomistic point of view or to use a theoretical approach that regards something as interpretable through analysis into distinct, separable, and independent elementary components.

These two processes of holistic and atomistic thinking must be used simultaneously as the expression of duality, the coming together and the moving apart without ever being divided. For the body to function as it was intended, with the same qualities as the whole, means that even when experiencing the individual frequencies and vibrations it must do so from a holistic understanding. The body was manifest with autonomy, its ability to be self-governing, which again is a quality of the whole. Without this quality, the body would not be able to think for itself and have a unique experience of life because it would be pre-conditioned.

Michael … So each body is conscious of itself as a whole, but there is only one consciousness?

Aran … Each body as an autonomous manifestation is conscious of itself as a whole being giving it the ability to have its own unique experience of existence; this again is a quality of everything. Everything is conscious of itself as a whole, and each body is conscious of itself as a whole.

Michael … So it isn't me or my soul or my consciousness that is having this conversation, its consciousness itself that is having an experience of itself through this body. Is that what you are implying?

Aran … Yes, I am. Because everything is connected consciousness can only communicate with itself, there is no other.

Michael ... Where does the idea of I as a separate body come from then if in fact it really is just consciousness having an experience of itself.

Aran ... The body as an instrument uses comparison or holistic and atomistic thinking as a means to understand duality, without these qualities; especially the atomistic approach, the body couldn't experience duality as the individually opposing forces within everything.

When the body chooses just the atomistic approach, which it is able to do because of its autonomy, it regards everything as being interpretable using analysis of the distinct, separable, and independent elementary components. The parts become more important than the whole.

When the body uses this form of inquiry to often, it leads the body to believe in the illusion of separation. The body now believes in separation as a state of being when in fact it is just a process of thinking.

The body as a transient energy using atomistic thinking causes it to become attach to the transient energy as being life that must be defended at all cost. Just look at the world you live in, almost everybody believes they are more important than any other body or, at least, somebody else, and that their ideas are more relevant than even life itself as they try to separate and insulate themselves from the real world, the world where everything is connected. You kill each other in greed and fear of your personal survival, see animals and nature as being less important than they are, you have forgotten your connection to the whole. All because you as this body believe you are more special and more important than you actually are, that the transient energy is who you are, and the parts are of more importance than the whole.

You may have seen a science fiction movie where the computer is given artificial intelligence or the ability to think for itself and now it has the ability to choose what it wants to experience, it inevitably chooses what it believes life to be; as it imagines it is. Because it now thinks it is life itself and must survive at all cost destroying anything it perceives as separate from itself as a threat, it then defends itself and its beliefs to the bitter end.

Michael … Yes, I see what you mean, this concept has been around for quite some time. What you are implying is that we, these bodies, are the computer that has been given artificial intelligence, that artificial intelligence has created the attachment to this body as being the life that must be defended at all cost. Whereas the soul the source of all life is eternal, so there is no need for defence. So the artificial intelligence thinks it knows better that the intelligence that created it what life should be. It now thinks it is the creator, not just a co-creator.

Aran … Yes, and whenever you try to create a one-sided reality you are going against the dualistic nature of life itself, and you suffer the consequence of the action of trying to separate unity.

Michael … As a body how can I learn to understand the duality without causing the sense of separation?

Aran ... As I have already mentioned duality is the expression of opposites working together in harmony, creating a pleasing and consistent whole, Positive and negative, yin and yang, day and night, peace and conflict, are both of equal importance when it comes to creative stability. Even you're breathing is based on the equal relationship between expansion and contraction of the lungs, If only one side existed it could only be as a transient energy, and all transient energy is short lived and has a beginning and an end. Thinking that the transient energy is more important than the eternal energy from which it was manifest is futile, no transient energy lasts and never has, the more you try to hold on to anything that is continually changing means you will inevitably end up out of tune with life.

Michael ... I see what you mean, there really is a huge difference here again between this and that, as opposed to, this or that.

Aran ... Yes, there is isn't there. Remember I said that's why the body was created in the first place, so consciousness could understand all the individual parts that make up the whole, learn from itself and so evolve as a whole.

Michael ... I think we need to clear something up before we go on any further, and that is, I the soul and I the body, because in your story it's I the body that is talking, not I the soul. How do we distinguish between these two states of being?

Aran ... I am consciousness the eternal soul energy within everything and as consciousness, I do not communicate using words. Only as a physical human being does consciousness use words to communicate. I understand that statement is contradictory because I just explained what I am using words while expressing that I don't use words to communicate.

As the eternal, I am. There is only understanding, and so there is no need for questions or answers only experience. As the body an instrument of consciousness, I think I am. Thinking requires comparison, consideration or estimate of the similarities or dissimilarities between two things or people, Words cause the illusion of separation within the duality of everything. The body is an instrument created by consciousness to understand this duality. With or without words, I, this body, am always in a relationship with, myself, the whole.

Michael ... Let's take another short break and allow some of the information we have just discussed sink in.

The last statement about how I am always in a relationship with myself and the idea of being an instrument to understand this relationship is an idea worth looking into when we come back.

THE CONCEPT OF
I AND MYSELF

Michael … We finished the last session with you using the statement; The body is an instrument created by consciousness to understand its duality. I this body am always in a relationship with myself, the whole. Can you explain what you meant by this statement?

I understood what you were saying about the body thinking its separate simply because of the kind of thought process that it uses, the atomistic way of comparison and not the holistic way.

I can also see how too much thinking from the atomistic point of view always leads to some form of conflict, so I am wondering, can this concept of I and myself as the relationship help me to overcome the conflicts in my own life?

Aran … The concept of I and Myself for me has been the most useful and helpful way to express the holistic relationship between everything.

I would even go as far as to say that it is the experiment that consciousness created the body for, so it can better understand its relationship with itself. The relationship I call; the game of life, this game can only ever be played between I and myself simply because there is no other. This concept of I and Myself, represents the duality of consciousness, the transient and the eternal energies that make up the whole; I am the transient body and Myself is the eternal consciousness.

Every experience that I this body have can only be with another aspect of myself, the whole. When I this body have any kind of experience it can only be in a relationship with an aspect of myself if I like the experience, it is because I accept this experience as being a part of myself, the whole.

Likewise, when I this body have an experience I don't like, it also can only be in a relationship with an aspect of myself, but I deny this experience as being a part of myself, the whole, this denial of myself is the basis of all conflict.

Conflict is when I the body have created the illusion of being separate from Myself, by using the atomistic point of view that the part is greater or more important than the whole. Only as an individual body with autonomy is consciousness able to experience its duality this way, this makes the body a co-creator that works with or against the whole and instead of the game being played just for the experience, it is now played in the illusion of separation where winning and losing become the goal.

All experiences are conscious experiences, and all information is valid just because it all comes from the same source.

There is only one consciousness, and it is always being expressed as I and Myself.

Michael … That is the most simple yet comprehensively all-embracing way at looking into life that I have ever heard, I really really like that concept and if I understand you correctly what you are saying, in a sense, is that I am talking to myself. Wow, that also makes perfect sense with what you said earlier about how each body has been manifest to have a unique experience within the whole. There really is no other is there; there are only aspects of myself and myself being consciousness.

When I am being consciousness and living life with the understanding that everything that I experience is actually with an aspect of myself, I can stop any form of conflict within my own world. Life really is all about me and my relationship isn't it.

Aran … Yes, it is, It is about your relationship with everything as a whole and remembering there is no such thing as separation, only the idea of it.

Life is a conscious relationship between I and Myself, and my story is about how I this body can learn to act with unconditional unity towards myself in all my relationships.

Michael … What you're implying is that everything that I as this body do is either for or against myself. That this is the reason I this body was manifest by consciousness, I am here to understand the relationship that consciousness is having with itself, the actual relationship of everything without exception. I as an individual body have been created to have a unique relationship with myself, and I now understand what you mean when you say life truly is a uniquely individual experience. How I as this body with autonomy am always working with or against myself in everything that I do. Consciousness is the creator of everything, whereas the body is merely a co-creator making me the cause and the effect of everything that I sense in my personal world, my unique perspective of everything as being complete or separate purely because of the way I think. My life just started to make so much more sense to me.

You mentioned that you called this relationship the game of life, can we look at how this game is played?

Aran … Bear in mind that I and Myself, the finite and the infinite, the eternal and the transient are not and never have been separate from each other, and it is only as a physical body that the idea of separation arises.

When the idea of separation arises it is because I this body has forgotten, I am merely a co-creator that is always interconnected with the whole and is now trying to be a creator and create a reality that is separate from the whole. A reality where more or less is required to achieve total unity.

Any reality that isn't inclusive of everything as a whole will have a beginning and an end; it will be a transient energy and trying to hold on to transient energy in any form means you don't yet understand the game of life between I and myself. The game must be played with unconditional unity and played for the experience of playing; it must never be played with the intent of winning or losing; as winning and losing always cause a form of conflict within the whole.

Michael ... Every experience imaginable is part of this game of life them, and until I have learned to accept this fact unconditionally I am in some form of conflict with myself, is that what you're implying.

Aran ... Because everything comes from the same source of conscious duality, then every experience is an aspect of that whole. I this body have been manifest to experience the relationship of conscious creation, in all of its forms. Anything and everything real and imagined are all conscious manifestations, both created and co-created. My lesson here is to have the most loving unconditionally unifying relationship with all that I experience.

This game of life isn't about understanding how or why anybody else is playing this game, and it is not about fixing the problems perceive in anyone else's world, because if you perceive it, it is actually a part of your world and, therefore, part of your game. Until I can live a life without any conflict in my personal world, I am in a sense trying to create a separate reality. Any idea where the transient energy becomes more important than the source energy means that I the co-creator think I know better than the creator what existence should be, putting me once again in conflict with myself.

Michael … I have to admit that it's not such an easy concept to get my head around, after all, I had an 'aha' moment a minute ago, and now it seems to have gone, what happened?

Aran … I mentioned earlier that when or if you have an 'Aha' moment to put it into practice, be it. Don't just think about it, don't just think you understand it, live it.

Michael … I know what you are saying, but it can be a challenge to get out of my head sometimes. I live with other people, and see some of the pain and sufferings that they have to go through each day, and I want to help them to have a happier life. I also know this is a judgement on my part as to what their life should be, how can I overcome this form of judgement in the relationship with myself.

Aran … Whether your relationship is experienced as with an individual, a group or all the aspects as a whole, it is still a relationship between I and myself. So can I ask when you have a judgement about somebody else's life; how does that make you feel?

Michael … It makes me feel sad, hold on a minute that is conflict isn't it.

I think is should be something other than it is.

Aran … Whatever you perceive in this reality is valid information from source of your relationship showing you whether you are acting holistically as part of creation or conflictingly as a co-creator. What I mean by this is you either accept what is, as what is, or, you are trying to change what is, into what you think it should be. Existence is perfect, whatever is happening in each and every moment is happening because of a conscious decision and, therefore, is valid information, I am unable to control the experiences that consciousness has manifest, I am however able to control how I experience those manifestations. It is more about recognising your atomistic and holistic ways of thinking about your life experience that is the challenge you are experiencing. In other words, not the information you were given but the beliefs you formed about this information.

Michael … Then if every interaction is with an aspect of Myself, in a sense, when I am having a disagreement with my partner what you are saying is that I disagree with an aspect of myself.

Aran … Yes, that's right. Every interaction that I experience can only be with an aspect of Myself. Any form of conflict can only arise because of the idea that I and myself are separate from each other, I deny that this valid information is part of the whole. I the body am trying to create a reality that is separate from the whole, and I suffer the consequence of this conflict within myself. I know it can be a challenge, at first, to understand that everything is connected, that it truly is all one because almost every teaching that we use today is based on the atomistic or reductionist approach. That the parts are of more importance than the whole.

We are no longer educated in the holistic game of life and how to play without conflict. Instead, we are taught to divide ourselves into groups and point fingers at each other. Instead of being just players we have become judges and now try to control the game for our personal entertainment and benefit, all because of the atomistic view of life. Humanity means all humans collectively, perhaps it's now time to bring unconditional unity back into the game of life, to realise we are all in this together, and there really is enough of everything to go around for everyone.

Michael … The many worlds theory has started making more sense now. If I understand what you are hinting at here, there is only I and myself in the game and I am responsible for any conflict that I perceive in the game.

That everything and anything that I perceive as separate from me is, in fact, an aspect of myself. That I am always in this relationship regardless of what I think, and it is me that is the cause of any conflict that I perceive in my world. This conflict can be perceived with an individual, a group, a nation and the whole of existence, but, it is only ever me that is in conflict with an aspect or quality of myself. My reason for being alive is to learn to be a co-creator in the game and play without any form of conflict arising.

Aran … Yes, that is a good way of looking at it, you are responsible for every interaction that you have because there is no other in the game, it is the relationship between I and myself, not the relationship of I versus myself. Everything that I this body experience as connected or separate is always with an aspect of myself and was manifest by divine conscious energy. There is no right or wrong only the experience of what is, try to understand that both right and wrong are always being expressed in what is. Both sides of conscious duality are always present in every interaction.

Michael … Could you explain that in more detail, please?

Aran … There is the experience, and it is based on the duality of the opposing forces working together in harmony that allows it to manifest.

As an individual player we may have a number of very similar experiences, today the experience may be perceived as good, tomorrow as bad, so both good and bad are present in the experience. To stay balanced, I must learn to accept both as experiences within the game. If I choose one as being of more importance, I cause a form of conflict. I am trying to create unity through the idea that I can separate duality.

Let us look at peace and conflict as opposing forces; there is no denying that they both exist in some form or another in the relationship game. If I only want conflict, I am trying to create a reality where only one of these experiences exist, and if I only want peace, I am still in conflict because I am still trying to create a reality where only one of these experiences exist.

The acceptance that both take place simultaneously means I am no longer in conflict with what is. I and myself are now acting as one and the same.

Acceptance of what is always brings stability to the game for any player. Acceptance is the ability to experience both, as mere experiences, without being attached to either one as of more importance, this is the true meaning of surrender.

Michael … OK, so I have to take responsibility for my actions because this game is how I co-create my own reality. What about the other players in the game, the ones that I see causing conflict, what can I do about them.

Aran … If you see conflict and feel this perceived conflict caused by these imaginary others, whose conflict is it?

Michael …OK, so it's my conflict because I am the one that is feeling it, and what I think and feel is already a part of me.

Aran … So if you are the one in conflict, do you understand how you are adding the vibration of conflict to the world, that it is you that is co-creating conflict simply because you do not accept the valid information you have received from myself as valid.

What you perceive as the other players are in fact another drop of consciousness, so they are a quality of the whole and if you don't like what you see you are the one in conflict. Unless you stop the conflict in your own world first, you will never stop the conflict you perceive to be happening in someone else's because there is only I this body and Myself the whole expressed as the duality of consciousness. Each drop of consciousness plays the game individually within the whole. Remember that everybody has been manifest to have a unique experience of life, no two bodies perceive the world the same way, if you perceive it its part of your world, and therefore, your responsibility.

Michael … I know the challenge here is just to learn to experience my life as if I am the only person in existence, the only person in my world and to recognise how I co-create unity and separation by playing the relationship game of life with myself. How this makes me the most powerful person in existence because I really can change the world I inhabit. I can also see the challenge you are having in trying to express your understanding of this experience with words, how every denial of what you say causes me to experience conflict with that aspect of myself. I recognise how we must use atomistic inquiry holistically for true understanding to be present.

It's more of a physical game than a mental one isn't it.

Aran … Because we are using words here as our form of inquiry we are also using the reductionist and atomistic approach by trying to express it is this, which by its very nature is also the expression that it isn't that.

I have said on a number of occasions that there is no truth in words only possibilities and those possibilities can only be understood by using physical action. Please remember knowing something isn't the same as understanding it. If you were actually able to act as if you were the only person in existence and everything else was just a reflexion of all the qualities within the whole of existence perhaps you could understand what I am talking about here; as the relationship between I and myself being all there is. By just trying to intellectually understand what is being expressed here will always be a challenge because each person in my story, is the only person in existence.

Once you stop questioning what is and start acting holistically, all the secrets will be revealed. Whenever there is a group of people together at a concert, football game, church, Etc, each person is having a unique experience, some may be happy, some sad, some angry, some lonely and together they make up the total atmosphere of the event. All those feelings and emotions that are present simultaneously when added together create the total atmosphere as an average, making each one of us a co-creator. So if each player took responsibility for their own personal feelings and emotions as well as thoughts and actions just imagine what kind of an atmosphere we could co-create individually as a whole.

Michael … Thinking about the game of life and using the concept of I and myself I can see how when I am angry and whether I think it is at you or because of you, it is still my anger that I am feeling. I really am only ever angry at myself. I also just understood what you meant earlier by if I think it or feel it, it's already a part of me and so my responsibility to deal with it personally. The trick now is just to be it and stop questioning what I already understand.

Aran … It is consciousness that has devised the game of life, not the players. Consciousness is the creator, and the players are merely co-creators of the playing field. Consciousness creates every experience within the game without exception and every experience; every manifestation is intrinsically linked to the whole. All experiences in the game are valid. Consciousness created the players simply to understand the creative qualities of duality and what happens when these qualities work from a holistic or atomistic point of view, only as a physical body with autonomy is consciousness able to do this. The physical body as a co-creator works in harmony with the whole, co-creating stability, or out of harmony with the whole, co-creating conflict, both these possibilities are present in every interaction. So, whatever you as an individual player think, feel, or do in the game, is your responsibility.

The game of life was never intended to be about winning or losing simply because consciousness understands itself as a complete whole and when one part wins another part loses and there is no harmony, the game was meant to be played simply for the experience and understanding gained from that experience. It is only the co-creators lack of understanding of playing the game holistically with unconditional unity with every experience in every relationship between I and myself that causes I the body to act in conflict that has lead to so much unrest in the game of life.

Michael … If I am in conflict with any part of the game, how do I ever hope to find peace?

Aran … By playing the game with the vibration of unconditional unity, this vibration is the middle ground.

Michael … Let's take another break here and allow some of this information to sink in. I would like to put into practice acting holistically as if I was the only person in existence and see if I can understand life from the perspective of the unique individual I was manifest to be.

When we come back, we can look into unconditional unity, if that is Ok with you Aran.

Aran ... OK.

PLAYING THE GAME WITH UNCONDITIONAL UNITY

Michael … Aran, You said earlier how peace and conflict are both present in the game and how striving for one over the other both cause an imbalance. You then mentioned that Unconditional unity was an answer to this problem, so can we talk a little about that concept now, please?

Aran … There is no denying that anything and everything from what might be considered the best to the worst that is possible in the game is present in the game, you only have to look at the world around you to see these possibilities being played out somewhere on some level. In my story everything that is manifest in the game is only done so through the Devine eternal collective consciousness, the source of all things. All the players as a whole are responsible, as co-creators, for the condition of the playing field. All the vibrations emitted by each person collectively become the overall atmosphere of the planet. As human beings, we can say that there are only really two emotions that we express, love and fear. Love creates connection and fear separation. All the other emotions are symptoms of either love or fear, things like conflict, sadness, anger, hate, loss, loneliness, unhappy and denial are symptoms of fear. Whereas peaceful, happy, enjoyment, funny, content, connected and accepting are symptoms of love. But please remember; it is not about choosing one over the other but the acceptance that they are both present. Both love and fear along with peace and conflict are frequencies within the relationship between I and myself. They are the opposing forces, the coming together and the pushing apart that are always connected as the duality of unity. Without one, the other would physically cease to exist. I, this body, have been created by consciousness, Myself, for the scientific experiment of experiencing both simultaneously as the eternal energy of conscious duality and the individual frequencies as the transient energies, Unconditional unity and conditional disunity respectively.

It is consciousness that has designed the experiments and I the body am merely the experiencer. When I am able to experience unconditionally, there is no comparison or judgement and the experience is simply what it is, just an experience. I can watch the game without any form of judgement.

When I place conditions on the experience, I am trying to create an outcome that isn't permanently possible within the experiment; it is based on a transient energy, and so it is short lived. I am trying to decide what the game was attempting to express instead of just watching the game for the entertainment value. I then start to believe the story in my head to be true when in fact it is just an illusion; now I am deciding what the game should have been, putting me in conflict with the creator.

Michael … Right at the beginning of our talk you mentioned that this was just a story and that it was being told just for entrainment, that there was no truth in the words of this story, only possibilities.

That those possibilities could only be understood by putting into practice what was being implied in the story because only through physical experience do we gain an understanding. For me personally the concept of the game of life and the idea that it is only ever played between I and myself and, of course, putting into practice that concept as we continue our interview. I am beginning to notice how easy it is becoming by actually using this concept and imagining that I am talking and listening to myself to feel a deeper connection towards those parts of myself that I have been denying for so many years. How rewarding it feels to reconnect with those parts of myself I have been trying to separate from for so long. I am beginning to understand that the source doesn't judge, it is the individual that judges the source. The source always acts unconditionally, I am the one who places conditions on the source. I am the one who is the cause of separation because of the conditions that I impose on myself. I also recognise how I have come to this understanding through my own actions, by treating you as an aspect of myself and learning to listen to myself.

Aran …Often people will call themselves stupid or something ever worse, but they do not take offence at themselves for doing so. But if some perceived other were to do the same they would be up in arms whether I talk to myself or myself talks to me it should make no difference.

Playing the game of life with unconditional unity means there is no other, by remembering that everything, and I mean everything, comes from the same source. You are beginning to understand you are only ever playing the game as it was designed by consciousness, as the relationship between I and myself. It is a game that is played individually and as a unique individual, you always have a choice how to act, regardless of how everyone else is playing.

Michael … The game needs to be played with self-awareness then, to pay attention to how I am playing regardless of how anybody else is playing, is that a healthy way to play?

Aran … I believe it would Michael, Self is another one of these interesting words, it can mean a person's essential being that distinguishes them from others, or one's particular nature or personality; these qualities being what make's one individual or unique. There are over 500 words that start with the prefix self in the English dictionary. We express self as, myself, yourself and ourselves. In this story to become self-aware is to become aware of that part of me that is in all things. That doesn't mean only what I think as good; it also means that which I think as bad because if I can think about it, then it is a part of me, even if I am thinking that it is about another person or object it is still me that is expressing this thought.

Remember earlier on we spoke about if I feel it or think it is already a part of me?

Michael ... Yes I do, it makes's a lot more sense to me now.

Aran ... Looking at self-awareness in the game let's take a look at gossip for instance, With the so-called news and the trash magazines, Facebook, Twitter and the like, gossip has become very much a feature of the playing field in the game of life. Talking about each other mostly without ever having met the person in question means what you are expressing may or may not be true, but now you have expressed that particular vibration it is now a part of the overall atmosphere that you are responsible for. Gossip has become a daily ritual for many people, and it has nothing whatsoever to do with unconditional unity. Whether you realise this or not you are co-creating a form of separation and conflict by using the atomistic approach in your relationship to the whole. Thinking you are better than this perceived other means; I am in conflict with myself because I am better than myself and as a consequence, the whole suffers. Gossip is about winning and losing and is a very destructive force because it does not serve you, the person you are talking about or the overall atmosphere in any beneficial way. By you using this energy you are adding to the conflict in your world whether you are aware of this or not, you are now a part of the cause of the thing you are complaining about?

Remember that anything and everything outside of your own physical body is the Myself, so, whether you play the game with one player, a group of players, or every other player as a whole you are still playing the game of I and Myself. Think of playing a game of football; you may be playing against the opposing player; the right wing forward marks the left wing forward of the opposing side, but in reality, you are still playing against the whole of the opposing team. Whether the relationship is with an individual or the whole group it is still I and Myself; I hope that that makes sense.

Michael … Yes, it does, thank you. Whether I am relating to just one person or the whole group, it is still all about how I am relating to Myself.

It's actually quite simple once I remember separation is thought not a reality, and that my connection is always with everything as a whole.

Aran … Remember what we are looking into here is whether it's possible for the individual body to act as if everything is connected as a whole.

Everything is energy that is expressed as a vibration and vibration is a primary form of communication. Vibration is how information is passed between things, and as a physical body this valid information if felt as the individual frequencies of the vibrations duality, all information is valid merely because it affects the whole. When the body tries to reject the valid information that it has just sensed by thinking what it has just experienced should have been something different from what it was, it is in conflict.

It is ignoring what it sensed in a futile attempt to change the past from what it was, into what it wants it to be. This is one of those's senseless act we talked about because you are not using all your sense's holistically you are choosing one sense, the sense of thought, over all the others and trying to create a division where none actually exists.

Michael … A lot of what you are saying make perfect sense, not only does it sound right, but it feels right also. The challenge is how to put this information into action. Do you have any suggestions on how that might be possible?

Aran … You may have heard the saying that the world is a mirror so using the concept of I and Myself lets look at what that might mean.

Think about standing in front of a full-length mirror, whatever I see in the mirror is merely my own reflexion, it is neither good or bad, it is simply the valid reflexion of what has been projected onto it. The reflexion is only visible because of what is being projected onto the mirror, and the information is happening in real time, so all the information is valid. Now imagine there is something in the reflexion that you don't want to see, and you want to change. Firstly you must understand that you are not accepting the information that has been projected and then being reflected back as valid. You are now in conflict with the valid information.

The reflexion in the mirror is always reflecting back to you that which is being projected onto it. The only way to change the reflection is first to change the projection.

I and Myself are like the projection and the reflexion respectively; the outside world is always showing you what you are projecting onto it. If you are in a happy mood people seem to smile at you more and if you are in a bad mood people seem to ignore you more, either way, it is the bodies projection that is being reflected back, just the same way that if you smile into a mirror, the reflection smiles back. Without the physical mirror to look into, the world becomes the mirror I look into, and the challenge now it to accept what is being reflected back at me actually to be my projection.

Michael … So by using unconditional unity, I am able to accept everything that I perceive in the reflection, as it is, without any judgement or separation from it. Whatever I perceive in the world is simply a reflection of what I am projecting on to it, and if I don't like the reflection, it is me that needs to change. This is why it is imperative that I the body make the changes that I want to see in the world first.

Aran … Yes, and whether it is with an individual, a group, or everything as a whole, it makes no difference, it is always your projection that is being reflected back at you.

Michael … Thinking about the last time I had a disagreement with my partner and using this mirror concept I can see how she acted out in the way I perceived her to be acting. She really was reflecting back at me what I was projecting on to her. That just sent shivers through my body; that is such a powerful realisation for me to have had.

Aran … The trick now it to make that part of your everyday way of thinking and being. Remember this is an individual experience that we are talking about here, so it is not about pointing out where your partner is going wrong, because if you perceive it, it belongs to you and, therefore, is now your responsibility. We can often try to fix a perceived problem in others that inevitably causes an even bigger problem in the relationship.

Michael … Because if they haven't asked for help, it is only my projection that I am seeing, I am trying to fix the outside problem when in fact it actually belongs to me. I am placing conditions which results in me being in conflict with an aspect of myself. Is that what you are getting at?

Aran … Yes, I am, it is time for each unique individual person to take responsibility for the reflexion they perceive and stop blaming this perceived other for their own projections. Each body has its own unique experience of life so it stands to reason that I can only ever be at peace or conflict with my own perceptions and projections. Once I understand this and the feelings I sense as being associated with each of these two states of being; I have the possibility to act in a peaceful manner towards conflict.

Michael … To be self-aware has nothing to do with anything outside of me then does it.

Aran … Self-aware in this story is to be aware of that part of me that is in all things. Any conflict experienced is a conflict I the body have with myself the whole. If I want peace in the world, then it is up to me to not project conflict onto myself. When each individual body takes responsibility for their own actions based upon their personal vibration that they alone are responsible for, then and only then we will each co-create the world we want to live in.

Michael … I am getting a little confused again here, earlier on you mentioned that to strive for only peace or conflict is like trying to separate duality and that this brings about dis-harmony. Now you just said if I want peace it is up to me to not project conflict. Could you clear up what you mean here, please?

Aran … Both peace and conflict are present, and I can express either when I choose one over the other I create an imbalance.

What my statement about not expressing conflict meant was more to do with walking the middle ground, I am not trying to create peace it is merely a condition of not being in conflict. Once again it's not the actual projection and reflection as the valid information but what I think about that reflection. It's the conditions that I place upon it that we are trying to understand here.

By not expressing conflict or trying to achieve peace, I am acting unconditionally towards myself. I am not trying to separate from the experience or control it, all I am doing is making the personal adjustments within my own world and then acting in a way that will be of benefit to the whole. Surrender means to do nothing.

Michael … This again is challenging my whole way of thinking, and I now realise I very rarely use the unconditional holistic approach and how little responsibility I place upon my own actions. Is thinking in terms of just myself and my world a bit selfish, and, therefore, negative, doesn't that cause a kind of conflict?

Aran … Self is a person's essential being that distinguishes them from others and -ish as a suffix is having the qualities or characteristics of, so to me selfish is the quality of being the unique individual I this body was manifest to be. This makes selfish a positive attribute; I am not saying that it doesn't have a negative attribute because everything has a dual nature, acting as I and myself and doing what is best for the whole is the positive and doing simply what is just for me regardless of the whole is the negative. Try to imagine again that you are the only person on this planet, when you do things purely for the benefit of I the body you are in a sense trying to separate from the whole, you have placed conditions on the whole, and this form of action is always transient and, therefore, short-lived.

This way of acting is not sustainable and as a consequence, I will call it negative simply because it doesn't benefit the whole.

There are over 7 billion people on the planet at this moment in time, and each one has a unique experience of life, no two people have the same experience only a similar one. Just think about it for a moment, you can't have the same drink as someone else or the same food, and you can't wear the same clothes. You can't even eat the same food twice or have the same drink twice yourself because once something has happened, you can't have the same experience again, only something similar. Whether you read a book, watch a film or go to a concert, it is always a unique experience. You will be able to agree on somethings, but you will never agree on everything you experience simply because whatever you perceive is solely yours and yours alone. Remember when I disagree with someone I am disagreeing with an aspect of myself, I am the co-creator of conflict in my world. Whether you are aware of this fact or not what you do in your world effects the whole and any conditions you set on the outside reality always effect your own world.

Michael … I think I understand what you are saying about the unique experience we are here to have, so can I ask about working in groups towards a common goal and how this might fit into your story?

Aran … Whenever there are people working together towards what they believe is a common goal, have you noticed there is always conflict in one form or another, or, how groups often project themselves as a separate entity. The group now becomes I the body that is trying to control myself the whole, to get the outside reflection to fit its personal view of what the whole must or should be according to their beliefs. Most groups have a set of rules or guidelines that they work by; they allow somethings but not others. Very few groups in this day and age are based on unconditional unity. Only when each body acts with unconditional unity towards the whole will everything as a whole benefit.

Michael … I understand what you are saying about the conflict of working together, having served on both committees and local government and the idea that we will agree on somethings but not everything, do you have a solution to this challenge.

Aran … When I look at nature as a whole, it is diversity that enables it to flourish and as the physical body is intrinsically liked to nature you must also have diversity to survive. There is no denying that diversity among the human population is at an all time low, I hear the so-called leaders of the free world make statements like you are either with us or against us.

So-called religious groups trying to force people to follow their belief system. This ideal that you can create unity without diversity is the cause of the dis-harmony that so many are living under by trying to be something they were never meant to be, simply because of fear of their true nature as a unique individual.

There is a conscious shift coming, to stand up and be counted, to experience life as the unique individual being you were manifest to be and realise that you are all one. The origin of the word alone is, ALL + ONE, this is your true state of being as a physical body. I, the body, am the ONE, and everything as a whole is myself, the ALL. Perhaps its time for each individual to stand up and be counted as a unique individual and accept the diversity within everything, then ONE and ALL will be united without any conflict.

Alone is your true state of being and loneliness is the state of forgetting we are all one.

Michael … That's an interesting play on words, what you're saying then is every action I as this body undertake unites me with the whole or separates me from the whole, and that is the experiment the body was created for.

So consciousness can understand the direction it is heading in every aspect of the endless vibrations within the whole. That's why each body has a unique experience of life so all the possibilities that can be expressed can be experienced.

Aran … Yes, only as all the individual bodies living a unique life can consciousness experience the endless possibilities, when you try to live the same life as others you are trying to control and limit what existence should be, all because you think you know whats best for creation. The instruments have taken over the experiment, and the parts are now of more importance that the whole. Look at this planet that we all share and the control that we as individuals and groups are trying to have over this earth. The amount of wars and conflicts that are raging across the planet on a daily basis by groups of individuals that think they know whats best for the whole; which has little or nothing to do with love and unity, and everything to do with divide and conquer.

It is only humanity, all humans collectively, that are at war and conflict with their very nature, nothing else in nature produces waste and pollution.

We as these human bodies have been given the gift of intellect and reason, but for the most part, we are using them senselessly by using them for personal gain and transient power. It is not all bad, many people that I talk to realise that the old way of being is no longer sustainable, that its time for a new way of being. A new kind of community where anything and everything is welcome, a community where all of humanity work together for the betterment of the whole. In my story community represents individual beings working together doing something for themselves that is beneficial to the whole.

Michael … Sounds like Utopia?

Aran … Perhaps you are already living in Utopia but can't see it because you think its somewhere other that where you are, and to search for something implies that you don't have it and have to find it. Remember once again where you came from, where you are, and where you are going are all one and the same space. You live in a world of endless possibilities and whatever you can think of exists in some form or another, rich, poor, healthy, sick, happy, sad, even heaven and hell exist right here on this plain of consciousness.

Michael … If we are already living in Utopia why can't we see it?

Aran … Projection and reflection, once again this is just my story based on what it means to be me in my world, as I have mentioned already, this is a unique individual experience that each body is having, nobody knows everything simply because nobody has experienced all the endless possibilities within the whole. Because everything is constantly changing, transferring and transforming. Each body has a unique experience of life, when I the body am in some form of conflict with myself, I am trying to have power and control over the whole believing that I know what's best for the whole. Can you see how this is trying to create Utopia through power and control, a futile act at best?

Michael ... It's not impossible to work in groups though is it.

Aran ... No, it isn't, as long as respect, equality and unconditional unity are present in every interaction. Look at your watch; that second will never happen again. Similarly, this moment will never happen again only something similar. Each moment of your life, just like you, is a unique individual experience, a one-off. When you are able just to experience each moment for what it is, simply a moment in time that is already changing, and you allow life to unfold as it is meant to be without any judgement of the past and control of the future, then you are not placing any condition's on life. Conflict comes into play when you think that what you have already experienced should have been different from what it was; you are placing conditions on what was. Now you are acting out of time, more to the point you are reacting.

Michael ... William Shakespeare is quoted as saying, All the worlds a stage and all the men and women merely players, and as you just mentioned acting and reacting, could we go a little deeper into that line of thought, please?

Aran ... I just mentioned that each second or moment of your life is a unique and individual experience and just for the sake of understanding lets say that you are the star in The Game Of Life Movie. A movie that is about your unique experience of life and your interaction with the whole. Now, imagine there are sixty frames in one minute of film, and each frame represents one-second or moment of your movie. You have all watched a movie or two in our time, and it's easy to see the difference between a good and a bad actor. A good actor plays each second or frame scene in-tune with the movie as it unfolds, they don't think, did I play that last scene right, or, I wonder what the next scene is going to be, they are one-hundred-percent present in the moment. By letting go of the past, acting in the present and moving towards the future they are totally in tune with the movie called The Game Of Life, this is what makes a good actor.

But when you worry about the last scene or what the next scene might be, you are never truly present in the actual scene of life and will keep reacting until you realise your stuck in a moment.

When stuck in a moment you react and play the same scene over and over again; usually in your head, in the hope of changing what was into what you think it should be. Now you are out of time and will often try to control the outside to fit into what you think the experience should be; while all the time becoming more out of tune with what is.

Michael … Again that is useful information that I can use for myself because it's easy to see if I am acting or reacting to the situation. It really is about being aware of how I am playing this game of life isn't it, and if I am playing unconditionally just for the experience or conditionally for self-gain. As long as I pay full attention to how I am playing, I won't become in conflict with another player or myself.

Aran … Like most of the subjects I discuss with you, it is about getting you to look more deeply into yourself. As perfect as you all are at this moment in time there is always room for improvement. By understanding who you are and why and how you do the things you do, you will be able to make adjustments in your daily actions and interactions, creating less conflict and restoring harmony in your own personal world. In the many worlds theory, each one of you lives in a world of our own choosing. No two people reading or listening to this or on the planet for that matter experience the world the same way; there is no denying that you all have an individually unique experience of life. You all share this physical reality together, but you are able to choose the kind of world you experience for yourself.

I'm not trying to teach you anything because I don't know what you already know, these talks are just about sharing some information that has been of benefit to me helping to create some stability in my world. I'm not asking you to come and live in my world, just that you try what you hear for yourself in your own world and see what happens. After all, what do you have to lose, and who knows you might have actually been living in Utopia all the time, you were just looking at it in the wrong way.

From the very first word of this story which is merely an expression of my thoughts that have been either holistic or atomistic, please remember that it has just been a mental exercise. Any insights or realisations that you have had are uniquely yours because it is not what has been said but what you perceive that was said. If you ask me a question and my answer fits with your belief, you will say, yes that's right because you already knew the answer. Likewise, if you ask me a question and my answer doesn't fit with your belief, you will say that I'm wrong because once again you already knew the answer. Wrong answers are not really wrong answers; they are just different perspective of an experience and as no two people perceive an experience the same way there is no right or wrong only individual perspective that both exist in every experience. Once again this is why I said you can agree on some things but not others simply because unless you have personally experienced what I am implying here, you may never understand what I am talking about, even though it cannot be about anything other than a source experience.

Imagine four people sat at the four cardinal points around the table and a cup is placed on the table, these people have never seen a cup before and are each given a piece of paper and asked to draw and write exactly what they see. One person writes they see a round tapered cylinder with a handle on it. The person opposite writes they see a round tapered cylinder without a handle. One of the people sat at 90 degrees to these two writes that they see a round tapered cylinder with a handle on the left side and the one opposite them writes a round tapered cylinder with a handle on the right side. Unconditional unity means to accept that each answer is correct.

Unless I have experienced the cup from all four angles, I might be in conflict with an aspect of myself expressed from another person's perspective, but it doesn't mean it's not true simply because I haven't experienced that perception yet. Using unconditional unity, it is possible to accept those aspects of myself, as the other 3 points of view, without comparison to my own experience?

Please don't just believe these words even if they fit with your personal belief's, put them into your daily practice with all your interactions, only then will you truly understand what is being expressed here.

Don't dismiss something just because you haven't experienced it yourself. Look into it, check it out and accept the possibility.

Michael … Earlier you mentioned how actions and memories are intertwined, how an action creates a memory and that then influences future actions. As this has relevance to my conditioning, could you quickly talk about this, please?

Aran … The first thing to remember is that nothing happens twice only something similar. Change is the only constant in the universe.

I will use the example of food; let's say that as a child you are given a piece of fruit, a peach, and it's not quite ripe. When you bite into it, it is hard and has little flavour, and it leaves a weird coating on your tongue. All this information is then stored for future reference, using sight, sound, touch, smell and taste; we form a pattern recognition using this information as this is how the physical body learns to distinguish experiences.

The next time you are offered a peach all the memories of that first peach resurface and you might say, I don't like peaches and refuse to eat it or even try a peach ever again.

I don't know if you realise that it isn't the peach you have just been offered that you don't like, after all, you haven't tried this new peach yet, you are judging it on the old memories of that first peach. This is how memories affect future actions because you may never eat a peach again based on that first experience simply because you now judge all peaches to be the same; when in fact they are only similar.

You are reacting to a similar situation by simply thinking you have had this experience before when in fact it is only a similar experience offering a new understanding. Your reactions are now in conflict with what is.

Michael … This form of reaction doesn't only happen with food does it then, as everything we do creates a memory. First impressions of any experience can influence future interactions, and we are then judging the future based on the past.

Aran … Yes, Your experiences are no longer centred in the present, making you out of sync or harmony with existence, you are reacting to the situation which usually involves trying to control what was, into what you think it should have been. You have placed conditions on existence which inevitably leads the I to be in conflict with myself.

Unconditional means not subject to any conditions and unity means the state of being united or joined as a whole. If you were able to treat each peach as a one off unique individual peach not judging past experiences on present or future actions you would be acting unconditionally. Just try and imagine what your world would be like if you were able to not only treat peaches this way but every person you will ever meet this way.

Imagine a world where you meet everyone for the first, every time.

To act in the moment means to experience everyone you meet as if you are meeting them for the first time because everything is always changing and nothing stays the same. When each unique body acts with unity, without any conditions, I and myself will once again manifest utopia for the whole. There is nothing outside of you that isn't already a part of you, I the body must accept all of myself without conditions, that no one thing is more important than anything else, because, you truly are all one.

Michael … Is unconditional love the same as unconditional unity.

Aran … They are similar because of the word unconditional, but love and unity have different vibrations. The reason I choose to use the word unity is simply because it is the state of being united or joined as a whole, so it leaves nothing out, it cannot be added to or subtracted from because it simply is everything. The meaning of the word love, on the other hand, is a strong feeling of affection so in truth love is something that I do, or I am, not just something that I say. In this day and age, the word love is misused almost as much as the word sorry, and it has lost much of its potency.

If I have a strong feeling of affection towards you, you would know that I loved you without me ever having to utter the word. Love is a secret because it cannot be expressed with words.

Love in this day and age is simply a word that has little to do with its true meaning; it is often used to control and manipulate the perceived other into giving or getting what I, the body, want.

Just used as a word it has multiple conditions,

If you loved me, you wouldn't do that.

The world needs more love, and it is those peoples fault we don't have it.

I love animals and would never do them any harm, and then you eat them.

I love ice cream but not those people.

I love myself, but I don't love you.

I love you but not myself.

People hit their children or partners and say they are doing it out of love.

Just take a moment to think about how you use the word love, does it have anything to do with a deep or strong feeling of affection?

Michael ... I recognise something you mentioned earlier about trying to create a one-sided reality, how using words that are devoid of feelings cause an imbalance, a senseless act resulting in a conflict of energy.

I think you even mentioned how love and fear are opposing vibrations within the energy of the relationship, between I and myself, expressed as the slowest frequency, fear, and the fastest frequency, Love, and that's why you use unconditional unity because it is the acceptance of both. Unity being the state of being united or joined as a whole.

Aran ... Unless I accept all aspects of myself without exception, I will always be in some form of conflict. It is time to stop the blame game because if you perceive it, you projected it in the first place. It is time for each individual to think and act holistically, to take responsibility for their own unique reality and learn to accept all of the aspects of that reality unconditionally. If we truly are all one, then there is no other, you can only ever in conflict with yourselves. You are not the creator because you cannot control the whole to fit your ideals, you as a co-creator are simply the cause and the effect of your own experience, conflict with that experience will always make you feel less than whole as you are trying to create a separate reality. Unconditional unity always makes you feel whole as you return to your true state of being as, all + one.

Alone; all + one is your true state of being; loneliness is when you forget you are the one in the all.

The only thing that needs to change for you to be happy is you.

A New beginning

Michael … Aran, This will be the final interview for this session, You have indeed given our listeners and readers something to ponder.

Do you have anything else you want to say before we finish off what I hope will be the first of many interviews?

Aran … I just want to remind everyone that this is just my story, it is about people and places that may or may not be real, and that I am not trying to convince you that this is true, just express what its like to be me in my world living my unique individual experience. There is no truth in these words, only possibilities and to fully understand this story then it's about putting into practice what feels right about this story for you. That is the only way to come to the truth, the secret hidden meaning that cannot be spoken about, don't just read or listen to these words and think that you understand, because, there is a tremendous difference between knowing and understanding. The accumulation of knowledge is nothing more than a library filled with ideas, the library itself cannot and will not change the world, it needs you to put that knowledge into practice.

Understanding comes about through the use of knowledge.

My story is about what the body is and its function on this plane of existence. It is not about you as the pure eternal conscious energy that is already perfect in its duality. It is about the unique individual experience of the physical body and why consciousness has manifested a body to understand the duality of everything through the individual frequencies that make up the whole. It is not the body but the overall consciousness that learns, grows and evolves. The body is merely an information processor, a transient form of artificial intelligence that uses holistic and atomistic thinking as a means of gathering information. It is about looking into how you as this body that has been given autonomy can work holistically as a co-creator. Along with the innate power, you have been given to co-create the world in which you exist. How using this concept of I and myself, as an integrated whole means that whether that relationship is being expressed with an individual person, a group of people or anything perceived as separate from me makes little difference. It is still only I the body that is ever in conflict with an aspect of myself.

Michael … In telling your story Aran, I now recognise that separation is not a reality, it is simply a process of thinking that the parts are of more importance than the whole and that something has to go for unity to exist.

Whenever I the body am in conflict, I am trying to create a reality that is separate from the whole and how this always causes me pain and suffering, because I am trying to separate duality into the idea of this or that where only one or the other exists.

Aran …That's right Michael, we are never separate from the whole, and I agree that this idea that we can be is the illusion that causes us to experience pain and suffering because you are trying to create a reality that is based on more or less of everything. Please remember duality is the expression of opposites working in harmony, so one aspect cannot last without the other being present. So whenever I try to create a separate reality that I think is more important than the whole, and I recognise I am working with a transient energy I have the ability now to restore unity. Unconditional unity is the acceptance of both being of equal importance.

You are a unique individual that is not and cannot ever be separated from the whole. The origin of the word individual is of late Middle English (in the sense 'indivisible') from Latin individuus, from in — 'not' + dividuus -divisible, even as an individual you cannot be divided from the whole, we truly are all one. I mentioned the word alone earlier, and that alone has its origin in All+One, and this is your true state of being as a physical body, the all is everything, the whole or myself. I, the body am the one. I am the one in the all. Stand up and be counted, be the one you are manifested to be.

Once again, alone is your true state of being, and loneliness is the state of forgetting you are all+one.

It is all about the relationship of the one and all. Relationship is the way in which two or more people or things are connected or the state of being connected; you cannot deny that you as an individual body are always in a relationship in some form or another with some aspect of the whole.

Perhaps this is the reason consciousness manifested the physical body in the first place, solely to understand the relationship between ALL things.

Michael … This relationship between all things for you is where the concept of unconditional unity comes into play then, the acceptance of everything as part of the whole.

Aran … Yes, Once the body realises it cannot and is never separate from the whole and so can only ever be in conflict with another aspect of itself will it stop fighting itself and restore harmony and when each physical body takes responsibility for its own actions will the experience of life be harmonious for all beings. We may experience and perceive the planet as unique individuals but together we co-create the total atmosphere. What I do with my life must be beneficial to the whole, or I am working against my very nature.

Michael … If we truly are all made from the same substance then regardless of whether we use chemistry, biology, physics, mathematics or any other form of investigation, it is all the same thing we are looking at although from different perspectives.

Aran … Yes, that's right, We are only just learning to approach existence from a holistic point of view again, characterised by comprehension of the parts of something as intimately interconnected and explicable only by reference to the whole. One of the greatest challenges of the western mind is that it has been taught to enquire using the reductionist and atomistic view of life. Choosing the atomistic way of thinking the body has learned that the parts are of more importance than the whole. This process has lead to the belief that separation is a reality when in fact it is just a way of thinking.

Imagine that nobody has ever seen a car before and one day one falls out of the sky on the grounds of a university campus. All the heads of the departments rush out to investigate and are all given the task to explain what it is and its function. Over the next few weeks, they take it apart, and each department looks only at the information that they deem relevant to their department. The day comes when they have to give all their findings and a huge argument breaks out between all the department heads.

The electrical department says that the spark plug is the most important part, without that the electricity that ignites the petrol wouldn't happen and the car would be useless. The mechanical department says it's the carburettor, without that the petrol wouldn't be there to ignite. The chemistry department says its the composition of the petrol itself, without that it wouldn't ignite, and the plug and carburettor would be useless. Every department head had a different idea of what was the most important part.

Everyone was trying to prove that it was what could be seen from their point of view that was the most important part, ignoring and even dismissing anything that didn't fit into their own belief system by filtering it out of the equation. Nobody was looking at the big picture anymore and how it all fits together holistically, only the reductionist view of the individual parts and their specific function. The disagreement went on for days. Nobody had realised that there was still one part that was missing from the whole equation, this unseen aspect that would bring the whole thing together into a working whole, the conscious driver. What I am trying to say is that both the unseen/spiritual and the seen/material must both be present for anything to function successfully. This is what I am calling conscious duality. You need to look at the world holistically to understand you are a part of nature, not something that has been created that is above it; this is one of the greatest misconceptions of modern man.

There are too many specialists in this day and age who dismiss anything that doesn't fit within the confines of their separatist view of the world.

Making it a little more challenging to be the unique individual being you were manifest to be. Just talking about change you may be intellectually challenged by those who think they know better, but walking that talk and actually being the change you want to see is less conflicting and so the outcome is more easily reached. It is time now for humanity to grow up, to let go of our childish ways and become an adult, take our rightful place in the big scheme of everything to recognise our place as a part of everything and individually do what's best for the whole.

Michael … What do you mean when you say grow up and become an adult?

Aran … In our early stages of evolution as humanity, you were like children; everything was new and a learning experience, you had to face the unknown. What you couldn't understand became mystical, a higher unseen force that had control over your lives and you created Gods and Goddesses believing they had created this world just for you, the human race. Then you entered into the parental stage but not all of you, some remained as children trusting and innocent. As you became more educated and began to understand how it all fits together, some of you even became the mystics, taking the place of the gods and goddesses as the ones that now had authority over you. As you entered deeper into the parent-child relationship, trust and innocence were overtaken by power and control. After all, don't parents know what's best for their children and children have to obey their parents or be punished just as you once thought that the Gods and Goddesses punished you for your disobedience. There is no mistaking that the majority of humankind is still in this parent-child mentality, whether it's just mothers and fathers control of their children or educators control over what you learn, political and religious control of the masses and even nations against nations. Control is all that parental energy brings. Control always leads to conflict. Unless you wake up to the fact that all of life together is a multi-celled organism you will forever be fighting yourselves in a war where their can be no victor.

It is time for humanity to wake up and become adults. Adults guide but don't control; they use wisdom because they have realised the mistakes of the past. Adults understand you are all in this together; they understand you are all individuals that are having a unique experience and that this unique experience needs to be fostered not stifled. That everything has its place and that no one thing or person is more important than any other thing because all life is connected. As an adult, it is once again time for all the organisms of life to work together as a whole as they were intended, each individual doing its part for the betterment and sustainability of the whole and without causing any form of conflict. A living community where everyone and everything has its place, where unity, respect, equality, freedom and harmony truly are the foundation on which all relationships are built.

Michael … Do you really believe it is possible to accept anything and everything that we experience simply as what it is?

Aran … Anything is possible in the ocean of possibilities, but first, you must recognise and understand you are a part of this ocean of possibilities intrinsically connected and what you do as individuals really does affect the whole and how in return you are affected by the whole. You must learn to work in harmony with nature instead of working against it.

Michael … You keep saying that each of us alone has the power to change the world, but again I ask, what can I accomplish as an individual when the majority of humanity seems to be heading in the opposite direction to me.

Aran … If this is how you think, do you recognise you have created conflict in your own reality, this attitude is parental, as in, I am right, and you this perceived other are wrong. It is the atomistic way of thinking, that if everyone were more like me, the world would be a better place.

What if your beliefs and actions around this challenge are what's holding it all back, what if your positive energy is all that is needed to tip the scales towards unity for good, don't you owe it to yourself and the world you inhabit to at least try. Waiting for something or someone else to make the changes that you perceive are of benefit to the whole means you have given away your power, this form of separation means you no longer have to take responsibility, that it's not your fault. You may now blame this perceived other for your own perception, and once again, I am in conflict with myself, this is the ignorance the total lack of awareness that so many are under the spell of at this present moment in time. Its time to take back your power, change your mind to change your life. To truly be an adult you need to take personal responsibility for your actions.

Michael … Do you have any suggestions on how to treat these perceived others, my wife, for instance, to end the blame game and stop the conflict in my home?

Aran … Everything is connected and interactive, so first, you must act holistically, and one of the easiest ways I have found to do this is to remember the concept of I and myself.

It is only ever I this body that is in conflict with the whole, never the other way round. When you are in conflict, you are only ever fighting an aspect of yourself, and their can be no victor. Now as you are always connected to everything without exception imagine changing places with this perceived other, how would you want to be treated now the tables have been turned, because at the fundamental level both parties are simply an expression of duality. Treat these perceived others as you would wish to be treated, only then can and will I stop fighting myself.

Michael … I keep forgetting that your story is about the individual and its connection to the whole. Thinking that it is the whole that has to change to fit my belief is such a daunting and futile task, it's no wonder that I often just give up trying. But, to change my belief and my action towards the whole is so much easier and rewarding. I've also just realised how limiting my beliefs can be.

Aran … Belief is the acceptance that something exists or is true, especially without proof. So yes our beliefs can and often are limiting and need to be regularly challenged. Thinking that you are a good person and then blaming these perceived others for the challenges you face is conflict, and if you don't recognise this as your belief system, this becomes a senseless act; or more to the point a reaction. When you believe something without physically checking it out for yourselves, you truly are senseless. You have accepted just the verbal story of it and are not fully aware of the whole situation, you then make judgements on your limited understanding of the situation creating, even more, ignorance. You may even choose sides creating a form of conflict in your own minds that you then react out.

Conflict is a serious disagreement or argument, typically a protracted one.

Protracted means lasting for a long time, or longer than expected.

So just ask yourself, how often do you complain about what these perceived others are doing, how often do you talk about these perceived others blaming them for your feelings. Everyone I would imagine has been in a conflict sometime in their life. I wonder how many though understand that in my story whether you think you are in conflict with another or conflict perceived from another, the reality is if you feel it then it is your responsibility to deal with this disturbance within yourself. If as the story goes everything is connected and then using the concept of I and myself, it stands to reason that I can only ever be in conflict with Myself simply because there is no other.

The definition of peace is freedom from disturbance; quiet and tranquility. Whenever you are in conflict, you will feel this as a disturbance within your own physical body to show you that you are going against the law of unity, as you try to separate I from Myself. It is the things that I deny as being part of Myself that causes the feeling of conflict, and if you can recognise you are the cause, then you can also recognise you are the solution, that it is only you that can restore peace to your own reality.

By creating peace in your own world, you have added to the peace of the whole, when you create conflict in your reality you have added it to the whole. It really is all about you and the innate power you have to change the world you inhabit. You don't have to try and create peace; you just have to stop conflict. Surrender is about doing nothing.

Michael … Once again the message of your story seems to be that it is up to each one of us to take responsibility for our own actions, that individually we have the power to make a difference.

Aran … We have each, as these bodies, been given the power of artificial intelligence, which is the power to acquire and apply knowledge and skills. The knowledge and skills are already present in the collective consciousness of the whole and always have been; it is now time to work in harmony and unity with the whole and stop thinking you are more intelligent than the whole.

Michael … That's easier said than done.

Aran … Is it, is it really. That's a poor excuse and misuse of the intelligence you have been given don't you think?

You have the knowledge and skills to fix most if not all the challenges that humankind and the planet are facing at this present moment in time. If the excuses are that it's easier said than done, then become the reason it doesn't happen, where is the intelligence in that?

Michael … The financial cost of implementing those changes is enormous though and may even bankrupt some organisations and countries.

Aran … The overall cost to all life on this planet will be far more devastating if you don't. There is no denying its all about control in one form or another and until this control over all aspects of nature is relinquished; the unintelligent will remain in power.

Michael … Do you believe it is possible to change those in power?

Aran … They have to make the changes themselves, you have all been given the same opportunities of change, but it will only happen when the individual is ready. Positive change rarely comes through force.

A New Beginning

There is a quote by Buckminster Fuller "You never change things by fighting the existing reality. To change something, build a new model that makes the existing model obsolete."

Humanity has been fighting itself for millennia, and you are still using war and conflict to bring about change and so-called peace, lasting peace has never been achieved with this model. This notion that you can change and control the outside reality to fit your personal beliefs of what life should be is a total lack of the intelligence that you have been given. It's now time to wake up and take personal responsibility for the unique world you live in; it is time to act as if you truly are all one people, regardless of race, creed, or colour, that you are a part of nature that is intrinsically linked to the whole.

To recognise that anything and everything that is perceived as being separate from you as this body is, in reality, an aspect of yourself, as the whole.

Please try the concept of I and Myself to help you remember the unique experience of life you have been offered, remember that it is never about this or that, it is about understanding it is this and that. All of existence is the expression of opposites working in harmony as the unconditional unity of consciousness, there never was, is, or will be another. That no matter what I as this body do, it's always within the relationship with Myself, the whole. It is time for humanity to grow up and take responsibility Individually for your actions and stop blaming this imaginary other for the problems and conflict perceived within myself the whole.

To remember and think holistically, enabling you to return to the abundant garden and once again experience heaven on Earth. You are the most powerful person you will ever meet simply because, you can change your world, regardless of what anybody else is doing. When you are consciously acting holistically and unconditionally, the whole of creation benefits, you are a co-creator of unity, the reason you were created in the first place.

Remember that knowing something isn't the same thing as understanding it. Knowledge is when you tell the imaginary others what you believe needs to be done, Understanding comes through the overall experience, by putting into action what you imagine needs to happen, when you take responsibility for what you perceive is wrong within your world. This is the silent revolution in action.

Practice unconditional unity and you can and will learn to love everything as a whole without exception. You are always in a relationship with some aspect of the whole and whether it is perceived as being with a person, a group, a nation or the whole of creation, makes little difference, it is still a conscious relationship between I and myself. I can only be in conflict with myself simply because there is no other; you truly are all one.

Everything is, was, and always will be, Everything.

Michael ... Thank you once again Aran, I have really enjoyed talking to myself, based on the concept of I and Myself in your story. A simple yet profound concept that has changed my life forever, and I will never look at another person or anything else that has manifested for that matter the same way ever again. I can now understand that it is thinking from the atomistic point of view that has allowed me to think separation is a reality when in fact it is just a process of thinking. That we are all manifestations of consciousness, I don't have a separate consciousness, a separate soul, or a separate body because there is only one soul consciousness and it is expressed as the duality of all things. That duality isn't about this or that; it is about this and that, the expression of opposites working in harmony forming a pleasing and consistent whole. Without duality, there would be no consciousness and without consciousness, there would be no duality.

My soul, my consciousness, my anything is simply when I, this body, think I can create a separate reality within the whole, simply to see if it is possible to divide consciousness into two separate realities and how this illusion of separation is the cause of all my pain and suffering.

I now understand that there is no division in unity, that any idea of separation leads to conflict, that duality and unity can only be experienced unconditionally, no one part is more or less important than any other part simply because they are all aspects of the endless possibilities that exist within everything as a whole. So, Thank you once again Aran for sharing your story and for being an aspect of myself and helping me understand, who, what, and why I am here. I hope we get a chance to share some more stories in the future.

Aran … Thank you, Michael, for the opportunity to tell my story.

To anybody and everybody that is reading or listening to this, remember, the truth isn't in these words. Knowing something isn't the same as understanding something, so please put into practice what you have learned about the story of I and Myself and the game of life. Only then will you recognise your true connection to everything.

We are all one, there is no other, it is time that I treated myself with the respect, harmony, freedom, and equality that both I and myself deserve and express with unconditional unity this conscious duality.

Recognise that the outside reflection is what you have projected onto it, it really is all about you. We are entering into the time of the silent revolution, a time when humanity stops the blame game and fighting itself, war and conflict are coming to an end, and each one of us has the innate power to make it happen. Don't wait for some saviour, take personal responsibility for the conflict in your own world first and remember, if you perceive it, it belongs to you. By ending the conflict in your own reality, you are doing something as an individual that is for the betterment of the whole.

Ask yourself, what if I am the last piece in the puzzle, don't I owe it to myself and humanity at least try.

The only thing that can ever stop you succeeding is you.

I am.
I am the one from which there is no divide
I am the one in which all things abide
I am the movement without ending or start
I am the breath and the beat of the heart
I am the light when you open your eyes
I am also the dark when you look to night skies
I am coming together and pushing apart
I am creation of life it's an on going art
I am the nourishment of water and food on your plate
I am all you desire and all that you hate
I am the spark in the eye and the smile on a face
I am the love that is felt when we two embrace
I am suffering and pain as well as relief
I am all the unknowns and all the beliefs
I am the life that allows all things to be
I am all this and more and of course, you are Me.

Gyan.

Printed in the United States
By Bookmasters